SECOND E

Second Honeymoon

DAVE & JOYCE AMES

KINGSWAY PUBLICATIONS
EASTBOURNE

ISBN 0 86065 386 2

Unless otherwise indicated, biblical quotations are from
the New International Version, © New York International
Bible Society 1978.

AV = Authorized Version
crown copyright

Amplified = The Amplified Bible
Old Testament © Zondervan Publishing House
1962, 1964
New Testament © Lockman Foundation 1954, 1958

GNB = Good News Bible
© American Bible Society 1976

TLB = The Living Bible
© Tyndale House Publishers 1971

Front cover photo: David W Hamilton, The Image Bank
Illustrations: Nuprint Ltd

Printed in Great Britain for
KINGSWAY PUBLICATIONS LTD
1 St Anne's Road, Eastbourne, E Sussex BN21 3UN by
Clays Ltd, St Ives plc
Typeset by Nuprint Ltd, Harpenden, Herts

This book is dedicated to Joe and Brenda Hickok, without whose self-sacrificing ministry at Beck House we would be unable to hold Marriage Weekends, do marriage counselling or write on marriage.

Contents

Acknowledgements

We owe a great debt of gratitude to Bill Gothard of the Institute of Basic Youth Conflicts in the United States. Through his ministry our view of Scripture was greatly broadened. We were taken beyond a simple denominational doctrinal perspective to see basic life principles. He also served as a model for Bible teaching that goes beyond simple obedience into how to be obedient. Even Paul admits that the command to love our partners needs the support of nuts and bolts as he requires older women to *teach* younger women how to love their husbands.

It has been eleven years since we have attended one of his seminars but anyone who is familiar with his material will recognize a bit of Bill Gothard framework in Chapters 11 and 12, and we certainly want to acknowledge that.

Also we want to acknowledge the helpful co-operation of the organizations listed in the Appendix who conduct marriage weekends.

Joe and Brenda Hickok meticulously scrutinized the rough drafts of this book and lovingly pointed out sentences that just did not communicate and it was they who persuaded us to write the chapter on 'Meeting Needs', while Brian Abshire with his theological training made sure we avoided all the major heresies.

Since we write with a Dictaphone we rely quite heavily on typists like Vicki Contraras and Elisabeth Gauthier, but the bulk of the typing was done by a legal secretary, Diana Welstand, who spent many evenings at Beck House to make sure the product was produced.

Introduction

Traditionally, after the wedding, newly married couples spend a few days, or even a few weeks, away from the cares of the world in order to have an opportunity to get to know each other in a much more intimate way than they were able to during their courtship. Not too infrequently, couples who have been married five, ten, fifteen, or even twenty years will take a second honeymoon, hoping to get to know each other better now that the initial responsibilities of earning a living, setting up a home and raising a family have eased. However, many couples who take a second honeymoon never think about it in terms of this goal, of 'getting to know each other better'. They see it as a holiday without the pressures of work, family and other responsibilities. Without such a goal, a second honeymoon turns out to be nothing more than a private holiday. In the western world there are many organizations committed to enriching marriages which offer what one might term 'goal-oriented second honeymoon weekends'. Marriage Encounter, Christian Marriage Review, and our own Christian Marriage Weekends fall into this category.

Communication with one's partner is a high priority in any marriage ministry, because it is the life-blood of a relationship. However, when communication with one's partner becomes the top priority the marriage relationship is set up on a pedestal—which may at first sound good, but which raises problems. The reason this happens, even with some Christian organizations, is because Christianity is seen to be only one part of a total 'balanced' life. Under this view, it is quite understandable that, if you want to solve marriage problems, you look at everything else in the light of the marriage relationship and force it to fit around the marriage.

Western Christianity suffers greatly from being a privatized religion, that is, a faith which only affects one small area of life. This privatized Christianity attracts those individuals who find it difficult to apply Christianity to every area of their life. 'Total saturation Christianity', or a complete Christian world view, at first appears to be radical, fanatical and socially unacceptable in our secularized society. Consequently, anyone who approaches a marriage ministry intending to place Jesus Christ in the centre and show how his Lordship affects each area of life, is probably seen to be out of step with the times.

We certainly have a high regard for communication. It *is* the life-blood of a relationship. But there is another consideration—the truth of what is communicated. Children communicate well as they play fantasy games. They play house, cowboys-and-Indians and Star Wars, and act out their interpretation of the models in their home and on television. Teenagers have had nearly two decades to absorb and analyse the world around them. Occasionally their interpretation shows remarkable insight, but frequently it is only an advanced fantasy game. Unfortunately, many adults live out their lives in what is little more than a sophisticated fantasy game.

How do we go from fantasy games to credible communication? 'How can a young man keep his way pure? By living according to your [God's] word' (Ps 119:9).

This may sound simplistic, and we would be the first to admit that we have seen many use the Bible in a very simplistic way. But the fact remains that the Bible is a book of relationships. 2 Peter 1:3 states, 'His divine power has given us everything we need for life and godliness through our knowledge of him....' Everything? 2 Timothy 3:16–17 says, 'All Scripture is God-breathed and is useful for teaching, rebuking, correcting and training in righteousness, so that the man of God may be thoroughly equipped for every good work.'

The Bible teaches certain basic, 'non-optional' principles of life, so non-optional that, when violated, conflict is created in direct proportion to the violation. The Bible rebukes us by reflecting back our failure to live according to these principles. But it does not just leave us there. It gives another set of principles for correcting the conflict, and a further set still for training in righteousness so that the man (or woman) of God 'may be thoroughly equipped for *every* good work'.

We are not saying that 'all you need is Jesus' and that if you have Jesus your marriage problems are over, or, for that matter, that any problems are over. Jesus himself said, 'In this world you will have trouble. But take heart! I have overcome the world' (Jn 16:33). It is our relationship with the living Lord, and living according to his principles, that gives us the power and the insight to overcome life problems.

Problem marriages are not due to marriage problems as much as to a lack of understanding of scriptural principles. A poor commitment to personal holiness, or both. This last statement may sound like the simplistic babbling of a couple of uneducated Bible-thumping laymen. Consequently, we would like to call your attention to the words of Ph.D psychologist Lawrence J Crabb Jnr, in his (very excellent) book, *The Marriage Builder* (Zondervan, p.13):

I offer no simple solutions or proven formulas for the many problems created by living intimately with another sinner. However, commitment to the Lordship of Christ and the authority of the Scriptures will provide the needed motivation and strength to live responsibly. Responsible Christian living will gradually yield personal dividends of deep joy and unmistakable hope....Obedience to God will likely expose you to pain that could be avoided or at least numbed if your priority were 'to feel good'. When I face the choice of painful obedience or comfortable compromise, Peter's words often come to mind: 'Lord, to whom (else) shall we go? You have the words of eternal life' (Jn 6:68). The alternatives are following God or following our own preferences.

In the final analysis, communication will only have validity when both partners view the Bible as the final authority in determining the principles on which to conduct their life. While it is extremely important that both partners have the freedom to vent emotions that are completely a-scriptural, a successful philosophy of life cannot be developed apart from the principles in God's word. Not only is communication important in developing a life philosophy, but it is also important that a high level of communication be maintained and that we have the freedom to point out failure to live up to that philosophy. But there again, the word has much to say about speaking the truth in love.

Prior to conducting Christian Marriage Weekends, we did a fair amount of counselling with singles through the Christian servicemen's centre that we managed, but very little marriage counselling. Consequently, we cannot say that we designed the Christian Marriage Weekend from our experience as counsellors. The goal of our ministry has always been to make disciples, i.e. to help others to maturity in Christ. Discipleship training in the Lighted Laymen ministry has always carried a special emphasis on relationships. Naturally, it is desirable that disciples be able to handle the word of God effectively, share their testimony, share their faith, memorize Scripture, etc; but the only effective way of loving one's neighbour as oneself is through relationships, and we have always placed a high priority on teaching the relationship principles within the Bible. In fact, we have gone so far as to say that 90% of the Bible deals with interpersonal relationships, and that consequently 90% of the Bible is very interdenominational, or ecumenical. No one has ever made a denomination out of these principles. All the denominational differences are found in the other 10%.

We did our first Christian Marriage Weekend in September 1977 and it was very well received, but it had very slow beginnings because of other ministry commitments. As the impact of Christian Marriage Weekends began to make ever-widening circles, we were faced with more and more opportunities for marriage counselling. There is probably a principle some place that says that if you stand up and speak long enough in public about a certain topic, people will come to you privately to solve their problems in this area. Counselling has always been an integral part of discipling. Discipling is preventative counselling, and counselling is problem-oriented discipling, so the two are really inseparable.

Counselling has two ingredients. First, there are the basic principles which it is necessary to teach the counsellee to enable him to have an effective life. Second, there is the technique involved in helping the counsellee to build those principles into his life when he has already failed to do so. Our new (and totally unsolicited) counselling ministry naturally caused us to get as much training as we could on the technique side of counselling. This book, like our Christian Marriage Weekends, contains what we feel are the key principles involved in a marriage relationship. Today, if we were to design a Marriage Weekend based on our counselling experience, and cover those principles most frequently violated among couples who have problem marriages, we would have almost the identical Marriage Weekend that we started out with in 1977. Naturally, however, our experience has caused us to emphasize some areas more strongly than others, and we are constantly finding new ways to present old truths in a more effective way.

Surprisingly enough, most of the principles discussed on

the Marriage Weekends are not unique to marriage. This is due to the simple fact that married couples not only have a husband/wife relationship, but they also have a brother/sister relationship. Only about 25% of the material we present is unique to marriage (roles and differences, the Christian view of sex, etc), and we think it would be safe to say that these areas represent less than 25% of the counselling problems we are faced with.

This book is designed in the hope that couples will read it aloud together. We recognize that some couples find great difficulty in attending a Marriage Weekend, for various reasons, but we feel that those who will read a chapter together and discuss the points for consideration following the chapter, will receive a special blessing as they look at barriers to happiness from a very unique perspective.

Consider this: shortly after we are married, a topic arises that we discover is a very sensitive area. It may be in-laws, finances, or any number of things. The discussion does not go well. Maybe there is even a 'blow-up'. But we have learned one thing—we do not bring the topic up again. Consequently, a brick is laid. Another such episode, and another brick is laid. After five to seven years, a wall is developing. Then, on the Marriage Weekend, there comes an opportunity that you might not otherwise have. A third party presents the topic from a totally different angle and with scriptural insight. You don't have to suspect hidden motives because the topic is not being raised by your partner, but by Dave and Joyce Ames, a completely neutral couple, with no personal axe to grind and no hidden agenda. The subject is much easier to discuss when it is brought up in this way by a third party. It may or may not be fun, but there is a much higher chance that it will be successful. Many couples have shared with us that their walls came down over the weekend. They also found out how to keep from rebuilding them.

We know it will be hard to duplicate the atmosphere of a Christian Marriage Weekend, where you are away from children, telephones, and responsibilities, and quite naturally things cannot be written in a book in quite the way that they would be spoken in a seminar (it is more difficult to build in humour, if nothing else!). However, despite the fact that the material is presented differently, and the points for consideration are consequently different, you will still be doing exactly the same thing as couples on a Christian Marriage Weekend as they sit in the privacy of their own bedroom discussing the heart-issues of each presentation.

Many of the life illustrations in this book come from actual counselling cases. Most of them come from a survey we sent out to couples who have attended one of our Christian Marriage Weekends during the past eight years. One hundred and four couples responded, on average claiming over 36% improvement in their marriages. Approximately sixty of those who responded made statements on specific issues that were dealt with on the weekend. In most cases we have changed the names. However, to keep it from sounding like an anonymous case history file, whenever possible we used actual names, by permission. But just to let you know we are not treating marriage too clinically, we have included a lot of our own ups and downs as well.

One last consideration: we would like to tell you, as we would on a Marriage Weekend, that if one presentation causes you to become unstuck, we will be glad to chat with you. However, we realize this book will be sold far and wide, so Appendix A includes the address of the Association of Biblical Counsellors. Should you need to talk further, they may be able to put you in contact with a biblical counsellor in your area.

Chapter 1

What's On Your Agenda?

Counselling has proved to be a valuable feedback for us as we teach the biblical principles of relationships. It is sometimes easy to recognize cause-and-effect relationship principles in the Scriptures, to apply them in our lives and to teach this application to others. The fact that they are all God's truth and that they work 'as advertised' makes it very easy to overlook the obvious: that many couples who wish to improve their marriages frequently lack the proper scriptural motivation for doing so. One factor is that we live in an age where high technology has set us free from many of life's problems. Cars are more comfortable, homes are more comfortable, a lot of the problems with washing, ironing, cooking, house-cleaning, have been alleviated; we do not even have to get out of our chair to change the television channel. It is not difficult to see how the resulting mind set influences our view of the Scriptures. Why should not those who trust the Lord live a life that is healthy, wealthy and free of conflict? It is easy to forget that Jesus promised us that in this world we would have trouble (Jn 16:33).

In Christ we are accepted just as we are—mere sinners. But the Father has a goal for this relationship, and that is that we be conformed to the image of Jesus Christ (Romans 8:29). This is a goal of character development, and it has nothing to do with our personal comfort. We are all aware that not only is character not developed in some sort of trouble-free vacuum, it is not even demonstrated in such. When Jesus said, 'In this world you will have trouble', he went on to say, 'But take heart! *I* have overcome the world' (italics added). This means that our ability to overcome trouble is directly linked to our relationship with Christ. Consequently, our ability to live effective lives consists of more than just simply understanding the basic 'nuts and bolts' scriptural principles required to live such a life. There must also be a commitment to our relationship with Jesus Christ, and this must be the number one item on our agenda.

We learned years ago that one of the opening questions in a marriage counselling session had to be, 'What's on your agenda? Do you want to solve your problem, or do you want God's best for your life?' This is because God will not allow himself to be used simply as a problem-solver. Problems, in many instances, are like pain, which is a symptom and not the disease. Generally, the symptom signals failure to grow in one particular facet of our life. Sometimes it is a symptom of long-standing failure, and sometimes it is a stimulus for growth in new areas. No counsellor can guarantee a client that commitment to godliness will solve his problem, even though there is a high likelihood of it. But they cannot give much hope without it. No Christian counsellor would imply that commitment to godliness will produce a life free of conflict; but he can guarantee that being in the centre of God's will means living a life that is purposeful and victorious. Also, there is no guarantee that, if we live a life committed to godliness, our partner will do the same, because God will not force anyone into a life of obedience. However, one thing can be guaranteed: if two people live together committed to godliness, God will continue to draw them closer and closer together, because he is committed to marriage, as well as to conforming us to the image of his Son.

We fully realize that two unbelievers can have a successful marriage. So, obviously, two believers who are not
committed to godliness can also have a successful
marriage—successful by this world's standards. If we
believe that God is sovereign and that the first item on his
agenda is conforming us to the image of Christ, then we
must view each conflict, each pressure, and each disap-
pointment that he allows us to suffer as somehow related to
this character-shaping process. Therefore, the surest way
to capitalize on these apparent setbacks is to be in line with
God's will for our life.

There are several important reasons for taking this
apparently indirect approach to marriage success. The first
and foremost is that, if I am committed to developing the
character of Christ in my life, I will automatically become a
more giving person. Secondly, it gives us a positive, rather
than a negative, focus as we attempt to overcome our
shortcomings.

Ephesians 4 outlines a principle that is so basic that even
secular psychologists understand it. The overall emphasis
of the Bible is not simply to cease offensive behaviour, but
to focus on positive behaviour that will replace it. 'You were
taught, with regard to your former way of life, to put off
your old self, which is being corrupted by its deceitful
desires; to be made new in the attitude of your minds; and
to put on the new self, created to be like God in true
righteousness and holiness' (Eph 4:22–24). A very specific
example of this is quoted in Ephesians 4:29: 'Do not let any
unwholesome talk come out of your mouths, but only what
is helpful for building others up according to their needs,
that it may benefit those who listen.' In other words, the
tearer-downer must become a builder-upper; he must
become so preoccupied with his new goal of building others
up that tearing down is the farthest thing from his mind.

Many of us realize that we would be far better marriage
partners if less unwholesome talk came out of our mouths,
but to concentrate on what we desire *not* to do is to set it

continually before us, which tends to entrench the old habit, rather than rid us of it. However, when we decide on specific positive actions that we know are in line with God's overall agenda, we are assured of having the cooperation of God in developing these new strengths.

Also, without a proper agenda it is all too easy to lose sight of personal responsibility in a marriage relationship. In John 21, after Jesus had reinstated Peter and indicated that he would be martyred for his faith, Peter pointed to John and said, 'Lord, what about him?' Jesus answered, 'If I want him to remain alive until I return, what is that to you? *You* must follow me' (italics added). As we assess our marriage relationship it is all too easy to focus on what our partner ought to be doing. In fact, at the beginning of a Marriage Weekend we have to say something of this nature, for fear of having several cracked ribs as marriage partners jab each other with their elbow to say 'I hope you're paying attention.'

We realized long before we began to do Marriage Weekends that it was commitment to the Lordship of Christ that made successful marriage relationships—in fact, successful lives. And that it was as this commitment worked out in every area of life that life took on purpose and meaning. However, as time went on and we saw the wisdom and cause-and-effect relationship of the principles laid out in God's word, we saw how important it was to teach these principles. Unfortunately, the principles by themselves are merely a philosophy of life, and philosophies in and of themselves do not carry with them the power to execute them. And a focus on principles alone tends to be a focus on individual issues, causing us to lose sight of the overall picture.

Life is not lived by the mile, it is lived by the inch. And problems are not solved in the abstract, but in the concrete. When people come to us with marriage problems, we do not allow them to talk in generalities, because we must have specifics. There is no other way to untangle a knot except to

21

work on one loop at a time. It is also very easy to lose track of the overall picture while one is concentrating on single-strand issues.

John and Heather came to us after they had been married for four years. He was an accountant, she was a secretary. They had no children. They were members of a very live Anglican church, where they met each other as committed single Christians. The first two years of their marriage had been pretty good, but they admitted that during the second two they had had almost no relationship at all. They were 'married singles'. Their schedules had diverged until they had almost no time together. He complained that she was unaffectionate and bossy; she complained that he was a procrastinator and provided no leadership. We saw them six times, showed them the principles that they were violating, helped them to view each other from a much healthier perspective, and taught them to rearrange their schedules. We got them to where they were complimenting each other; they were becoming more affectionate and had a healthy sex life; he had assumed his responsibilities of headship and was fixing all the things around the house that he had been procrastinating about. The marriage counselling was effective. However, in a few short months they were right back in the same rut. They knew what they needed to do, but they lacked the power to do it purely and simply because they had allowed their spiritual life to go down the drain.

This counselling had been done on the recommendation of their vicar and as their vicar and house-group leader ministered to them and encouraged them, their spiritual strength returned and with this their ability to meet each other's needs. But even this revival did not last long, because it was dependent on an artificial life-support system, and not on the couple's own commitment to godliness.

On the other hand, we have counselled many couples who have tangled their lives up in a much more complicated way and have suffered much deeper hurts, and yet have been able to come through them. They have frequently come to us lacking bits of scriptural wisdom, but their success in rebuilding their marriages cannot be attributed to our giving them one or two missing pieces of the puzzle, but to the fact that the first item on their agenda has been to be God's man and God's woman. It is this that has equipped them successfully to plug in the missing pieces and to maintain this consistently.

For further consideration

Discuss the correlation between being committed to conformity to Christ and having an effective marriage.

Chapter 2

Love Is a Many Splendoured Thing

One of the songs from the musical *Oklahoma* states, 'Love and marriage...go together like a horse and carriage', and, I suppose, when you think of it in terms of word-associations, that is true. However, the song naively goes on to state, 'You can't have one without the other.' Unfortunately, too much of our thinking regarding love is borrowed from songwriters. Older love ballads may communicate a slightly more moral message, but their concept of love is as far from the truth as modern lyrics.

The song 'Some Enchanted Evening', from *South Pacific*, is as typical an example of romantic mythology as one could ask for. It tells us that happiness in life can be built on a glance from across a crowded room. The writer substantiates this reckless creed with the suggestion that love is a total enigma: 'Who can explain it, who can tell you why? Fools give you reasons, wise men never try.'

We certainly do not profess a thorough understanding of love, but there are some very substantial facts and biblical principles to guide us when the romantic aspect wears thin.

Love is the ultimate gauge of all Christian interaction. In 1 Corinthians 31:1–3 Paul rates it over spiritual gifts, knowledge, and even sacrifice. When the Lord was asked what was the greatest commandment, he replied, '"Love the Lord your God with all your heart and with all your soul and with all your mind." This is the first and greatest commandment. And the second is like it: "Love your neighbour as yourself."' And then he went on to make a highly significant statement—'All the Law and the Prophets hang on these two commandments' (Matt 22:36–40). A very free paraphrase of that last statement might be, 'If you don't understand anything else in the whole Bible, this is godly living in a nutshell—to have an effective love relationship with God, and an effective love relationship with your neighbour.'

It is also very clear that this love is a choice rather than an emotion, for the simple reason that it is put in the form of a commandment. We know of no place in the Bible where we are led to believe that God is holding us responsible for positive emotions towards anyone, but we are responsible for positive actions. It might not seem unreasonable for a God who is perfect to expect us to have positive emotions towards him, but that is not what the passage asks for. It asks for love, the same term that is used for 'love your enemies'.

Luke 6:27–31 states, 'But I tell you who hear me: Love your enemies, do good to those who hate you, bless those who curse you, pray for those who ill-treat you. If someone strikes you on the one cheek, turn to him the other also. If someone takes your cloak, do not stop him from taking your tunic. Give to everyone who asks you, and if anyone takes what belongs to you, do not demand it back. Do to others as you would have them do to you.' From these verses it is obvious that God is not concerned with our having positive emotions towards those who are trying to do us wrong, but that he requires us to have positive actions towards them. This passage has nothing to do with emotions, but everything to do with right actions.

Paul says, 'Love is patient, love is kind. It does not envy, it does not boast, it is not proud. It is not rude, it is not self-seeking, it is not easily angered, it keeps no record of wrongs. Love does not delight in evil but rejoices with the truth. It always protects, always trusts, always hopes, always perseveres. Love never fails' (1 Cor 13:4—8a). This definition also has nothing to do with emotions, but with right actions and positive character qualities.

Perhaps one of the reasons why songwriters tend to portray such a lopsided view of love is that it is just not a very specific word in the English language. In fact, it has become such an overworked word that it is downright flabby. The Greek language, on the other hand, has numerous words for love, which allows the people to communicate a reasonably specific message. The New Testament was originally written in Greek and by considering that language as it was used at that time we can gain some very specific insights into the intentions of the writers. We can thereby understand God's idea of love and the proper place for the different types of love.

There are three major Greek words for love and they should be part of every healthy Christian marriage: *eros*, *philia* and *agape*. Each one of these words we would translate simply as 'love', but each one has a very specific purpose.

Eros has the most physical connotation. It is a physical affinity, a physical desirability. It is the word we attach to sexual love. It is the root of the word 'erotic', meaning sensual pleasure. However, it is not always sexual, because not all physical desirability is necessarily sexual (unless you are a Freudian analyst, in which case everything is sexual). When considering physical attractiveness, many people would give a much higher priority to a pleasing face than a pleasing body. A young man may 'fall in love' with a young lady whose eyes are very attractive to him, and possibly only years later recognize that she has eyes just like his grandmother whom he greatly admired. *Eros* love always has its roots in physical desirability; something to be desired. It is the dynamic that makes a young man say, 'You float my boat.' It is the catalyst that seems to unlock some hidden 'chemistry'. But, chemistry or not, we see very little difference between this type of love and the affinity one

26

can have for classical cars, Chippendale furniture or old English cottages. Frequently, when driving down a country lane, we slow down or stop to admire a perfect example of an Elizabethan half-timbered cottage with herringbone bricks and thatched roof. This mechanism does not seem much different from our reaction to an attractive member of the opposite sex when we were sixteen.

Eros love is often thought of as sinful. In this, it has something in common with anger. But both are God-given devices to accomplish certain specific purposes in our lives. We are told to 'be angry and sin not'. The Bible also tells a middle-aged man to be satisfied with the wife of his youth. It is not the dynamic that is wrong, but how we handle it. It is also significant that the Greek god of love was called Eros, and he was the god which forgot all reason and will and discretion on the way to ecstasy. *Eros* love can be used or abused.

(Note: the word *eros* is a Greek word used at the time of writing the New Testament, but is not found in the New Testament. The New Testament simply does not address this subject at all. However, *eros* is reasonably synonymous with several Hebrew words which are used in Old Testament passages which do address this subject. (The biblical philosophy of *sexual* love will be discussed in detail in chapter 15.)

Philia is a psychological affinity. It is a friendship-love which is based on common tastes, common interests, as well as admirable and desirable qualities. Two people with different tastes and interests can work together towards a common goal and develop a strong *philia* relationship if they recognize how their differences complement each other. *Philia* love requires respect, whether it is respect that is somewhat self-centred, such as, 'You like Beethoven and I like Beethoven', or respect for qualities and perspectives which we ourselves do not have. It is this quality of respect in *philia* love that so dramatically separates it from *eros*. A young man may be attracted to a curvaceous feminine body which, from top to bottom, inch by inch, meets all his expectations; but he does not respect a curvaceous body. He just desires it. On further discovery, he may respect the discipline involved in maintaining the body at its present attractive dimensions, but there he is respecting a character quality. Abraham must have had tremendous respect for Sarah on that score; the Egyptians were so attracted to her beauty that he felt, for his own preservation, it would be best if he told the Pharaoh she was his sister, rather than his wife. He was afraid that Pharaoh would have him killed in order to get Sarah. The thing that is not always immediately clear when we read this story is that Sarah was sixty-five when this happened (Gen 12) and that Abraham had a similar problem when she was ninety (Gen 20).

Possibly the most detrimental dynamic in a *philia* relationship is a critical spirit. Our partners can have character qualities which are observed and admired by everyone around us, and yet we see only their shortcomings, which causes us to lose respect.

Agape is a motivational love. It is God's righteous love. We tend to think of it as a spiritual love, although this is not an accurate definition. There is, however, a definite reason for this which we will discuss later in this chapter. *Eros* love is described as an 'if', love: 'I'll love you if you meet my standards of attractiveness.' *Philia* is a 'because' love: 'I love you because I respect what you are.' But *agape* love is an 'in spite of' love: 'I love you in spite of the fact that you don't look the way I'd like you to look and I have difficulty in respecting you.'

One of the most important characteristics of *agape* love is that it is a righteous love. It can always be relied on to do the right thing to meet another individual's needs—not necessarily their wants, but their needs.

Agape love is rightly called 'God's love', not because God does not recognize, authorize and encourage *eros* and *philia* love, but because *eros* and *philia* love are responsive; *agape* is self-generated love. *Eros* and *philia* require some outward stimulation in order to respond; something positive must first be done to us before we can love back. *Agape* does not need this. The term 'self' in 'self-generated' is thus not an attempt on our part to take credit for a quality given to us by God, but explains the distinctive nature of *agape* love.

The world cannot understand self-generated love. Even the sacrifices of a mother are sometimes said to be traced back to her need to be seen to be a 'good mum'. This is basic humanism. Humanistically speaking, everything is thought to be at root selfish, because humanism sees the individual at the centre of his own universe. This is a very convenient philosophy, because it authorizes selfishness. It tells me I have no need to be anything other than selfish and I have a right 'to look out for old number one'.

However, if we view man as created in God's image, then even the unredeemed in his twisted state will still have some ability for self-generated love. (This statement, however, by no means implies that unredeemed man has some spark of divinity within him.) This ability for self-generated love can be demonstrated as we examine acts of heroism. Many unregenerate people have sacrificed their lives to save the lives of others. Stories have been told of men who have smothered a live hand grenade with their own body to save their fellow soldiers. The Bible tell us that 'Greater love has no-one than this, that he lay down his life for his friends' (Jn 15:13). So these stories describe definite acts of love which are not promoted or stimulated by outside forces.

However, we recognize that not even the redeemed are completely untwisted, and we find self-generated love more difficult in some areas than in others. God says, 'Love your neighbour as yourself', but we find that there are a lot of neighbours who are very difficult to love. The four-year-old next door comes over to play with ours; he is selfish, noisy, dirty, and worse of all, he seems to have a constant yellowish-green exudation running down his upper lip from his nose. Some people have no problem here; they just simply take a tissue and wipe his nose and gently correct his bad manners, and get on with loving him. But some of us lesser mortals realize that only God can love this child through us. This is another reason for calling it 'God's love', because we find that it cannot be *sustained* apart from God. We may have a certain capacity in a certain area, but our inconsistency shows us the frailty of our fallen condition, and we must call on the power of the risen Christ dwelling within us to do the right thing to meet another human being's needs.

Agape love is not, in itself, spiritual; it is a definite type and quality of love which God demands. All the statements in the Bible that tell us husbands should love wives, that we should love our neighbour as ourselves, and even love our enemies, are written in terms of *agape* love. It is not the love itself which is spiritual; it is the Spirit who provides the resource within us that enables us to love in that way. We have a tendency to mystify all the fruit of the Spirit and thereby complicate and sometimes annihilate our ability to communicate effectively on spiritual matters. For instance, joy is a fruit of the Spirit. To say that a Christian feels more joy at the funeral of a loved one than a pagan does when he has won the football pools, is ludicrous. The difference is not in the quality or amount, because joy is joy. The difference is that a Christian can have joy when a pagan cannot, because the Spirit is within, giving hope, which provides joy. If we say that there are two kinds of joy, then we have lost our ability to communicate a certain desired end result. If we talk about *agape* love in a mystical sense, forgetting that *agape* love is simply the ability to do the right thing in spite of our feelings, then it is too easy to forget what love is really all about. We may even come up with some silly excuse, saying or implying, 'The Spirit of God within me is not willing to love you right now, therefore I can't love you.'

Most unfortunately, all too often we spiritualize and mystify basic biblical truths in order to relieve ourselves of responsibility. The fact is that we are commanded to love, and we know that God empowers us to do those things he commands us to do.

Let us consider how these three types of love interact in a healthy marriage. Most romantic relationships begin with *eros* love—the songwriters' type of love. This is the attraction that sometimes tends to defy logic and certainly has great potential for 'love at first sight'. Sometimes people find they crave to be with someone they did not even know existed a few weeks before. *Eros* love is very exciting. But even secular psychologists agree that this type of relationship cannot sustain itself for more than three years at the most.

Figure I

Let the fountain in Figure I illustrate *eros* love. It is very attractive, shooting a column of water straight up into the air. This fountain has a pump, but no water source. It can continue to keep the column of water going into the air because the column falls back into the catch-basin and the water is recycled. The problem is that every little breath of air that comes along causes some drops of water to miss the catch-basin, and eventually the fountain runs dry.

A young couple may begin their relationship so physically attracted that they have a hard time keeping their hands off one another. Their courtship is very 'lovey-dovey'. Soon they find themselves in a biological chain of events which was designed to culminate in bed. They stop short of that because they are Christians, but most of their courtship is spent in as much romantic ecstasy as they think the Bible will allow.

Communication is stifled and the relationship suffers. This is because it is difficult to form words when your mouth is pressed up against someone else's. The fact is, they are only building a relationship on the physical sense; they are not learning about each other's character, temperament, likes, dislikes, fears, relations, goals and aspirations. When they do finally get married, they will wake up on the morning after their wedding with a total stranger.

She switches on Beethoven, and he wants country-and-western. His idea of relaxation is to flop in front of the television, and she wants to go out. He feels that his job in marriage is to earn money and hers is to pick up his clothes that he leaves strewn all over the house. After a while, they begin to realize the full impact of the statement, 'you can't live on love alone'. The wind is blowing the water from the fountain anywhere but in the catch basin. This was John

Figure II

and Heather's problem. They had done precious little to establish a relationship. After a couple of years there was no substance left in their *eros* love.

Joyce and I have found over the years that 98% of all sex problems are really relationship problems. It is difficult to give yourself in lovemaking to someone who is inconsiderate, has poor taste, or just generally seems to make your life miserable. Of the people who come to us with marital difficulties where sex is not the issue, we generally ask them how their sex life is, and it is almost always 'terrible'. *Eros* love will not sustain itself.

If the water will not stay in the catch-basin, we need a bigger catch-basin. This second fountain has a beauty all of its own. It has a second, much broader, catch-basin, and it has several little columns which recycle the water back up into the first catch-basin. This second basin is *philia* love. For many, this forms the complete unit. It is really all you need for a happy, effective marriage—as long as you do not get too strong a wind. If you have a lot in common, many admirable qualities, a positive focus and a reasonable amount of integrity, you can make it with just these two. However, since marriage involves cohabiting with another sinner, there are problems.

There are many couples who spend their courtship wisely and develop a sound friendship basis for their marriage—*philia* love. But unfortunately, even many of these couples wind up in the divorce courts. The winds of humanistic philosophy promote selfishness and militate against deep and effective relationships. Figure III includes *agape* love but there is a third, still larger, catch-basin and an even greater number of individual fountains to recycle the water. It also has with it one very revolutionary aspect. It is not merely recycling a limited amount of water. This fountain is connected to the mains. *Agape* love, with its focus on doing the right thing to meet needs, is able to resupply the marriage relationship when the substance of friendship begins to drain out, because its basis is firmly entrenched in

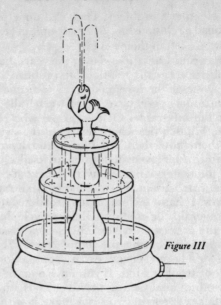

Figure III

God's rightness and love. This gives us a positive criterion for determining the direction of our lives when selfishness begins to drive us apart.

It is obvious that the most valuable component in this third fountain is the new base, *agape* love. This value judgement, although it is totally accurate, could lead us into error if we decide that because it is the most important, we can unscrew the other two basins and get rid of them. God certainly desires us to have the ability to develop relationships based on our mutual respect and compatibility. *Agape* love supports this. It enables the one being respected to have qualities worthy of respect. And it enables those of us respecting them to have a positive mind set in order to be able to see those qualities clearly, rather than just the areas in which they are failing. For instance, godliness is usually spelt with a small 'g' because it is not referring to God, but refers to a quality in someone who is committed to God. It does not take *agape* love on our part to be drawn to a truly godly person. Not only is the presence of God manifest in their life, but we also respect that person's commitment to godliness.

There is great danger in over-spiritualizing. If I, Dave, come home at night and Joyce says, 'Jesus in me loves you,' I have absolutely no security whatsoever in our relationship, because I also know that Jesus in her loves the little kid next door with the runny nose. So, frankly, that comment does not lift me up to greater heights. However, when she grabs me and says, 'I really feel for all those other women out there that don't have you (but not quite sorry enough to do anything about it)', that encourages me. *Philia* is the earthing of *agape* love. *Agape* love is the supernatural force which allows us to function effectively in a *philia* relationship.

God never intended us to function in relationships as though we were spending all our time swimming around in the bottom catch-basin of *agape* love. To do so means I have no responsibility to be attractive and desirable to my partner, and thereby to inspire *philia* love. God never intended us to live our lives as four-year-old runny-nosed children who absolutely require supernatural love. If I love my mate, I want to do everything possible to ensure that she has a bargain. I do not want to continually force my partner to rely on God's supernatural love in order to be able to live with me.

Every analogy and every diagram has its shortcomings. If we say that the *agape* basin is there to support the *philia* fountain, then one could conclude that those two are there just to support the *eros* dimension. But that is certainly not true. The meaning and purpose of marriage is not just to have a healthy sex life. However, just as *agape* love is earthed in a healthy *philia* relationship, a husband and wife have a God-given capacity for a physical expression of their *philia* relationship. It is not the most important dimension of a marriage, but it is something that we ignore at our peril.

The Bible limits sex—but it also celebrates sex. The Bible forbids the physical expression of a sexual relationship outside of marriage in order to protect its validity of expression within marriage. If God goes to such great lengths to protect and preserve this dimension of a relationship for marriage, then one can only conclude that it is important to marriage.

A few years back the head of a very well-known evangelical Bible college came along to a Christian Marriage Weekend with his wife. They had a very good marriage before they came on the Weekend. One would have thought that the only thing they could possibly gain from such a Weekend might be new ways of communicating the principles that they were already applying in their own relationship. Nonetheless, when they returned from the Weekend, it did not require a very discerning eye to see that something positive had taken place in their marriage. The survey that they returned to us for the purpose of this book gave the answer: they 'had forgotten the importance of sex'. It would seem clear from that response that *eros* love is not just an initial attracting device. It is a special dimension for warmth and intimacy, and as such deserves a certain priority.

However, as we hope we have illustrated, priority alone is not enough for effective romantic love. It must be based on a *philia* relationship, and that relationship, simply because we are sinners, requires the strong underpinning of God's love.

For further consideration

1. Is *agape* love a goal or a command? How does this relate to *philia* love?
2. What will it take to build a strong *philia* love?

Chapter 3

Seeing Myself Through God's Eyes

Psychologists tells us that by the time we are two years old 50% of our identity—50% of who we think we are—has developed; this has risen to 80% by the time we are six years old; and by the time we are ten years old, 99% of us have, to some extent, acquired a self-image problem—and only about 5% of us ever really get over that. So that would leave 94% of the population running around feeling in some way unhappy with themselves. Those figures may sound on the high side, but then, you have to remember, they are not saying that 94% are incapacitated through a low self-image, but that 94% have some trouble in this area.

After working with people over the years, trying to help them through their problems, our experience leads us to accept those figures as reasonably accurate. We cannot remember a counselling case where a poor self-image did not have some role to play. It was not always the major factor, but always an integral part of the problem.

Developing a biblical self-image is one of the key issues in developing biblical relationships. The way we view ourselves all too often influences the way we relate to others. For instance, John and Sarah Green told us that they realized, when they came on a Christian Marriage

Weekend, that they had a communication problem. What they had not realized was that a large part of the communication problem was due to Sarah's low self-image. She did not see herself as having much value, and therefore felt she had nothing of real value to contribute. On the Weekend she was made to realize her value in God's sight, and her unique worth as a person, as well as the value of what she had to contribute to their relationship. This enabled her to 'open up', which was the beginning of meaningful communication; and communication is the life-blood of a relationship.

Some have taken this concern for self-esteem to the conclusion that you cannot love another until you love yourself. Unfortunately this is even taught in Christian circles. But that statement cannot be backed up by the Bible. We are commanded to love one another and are therefore empowered to do so. From the passage in Matthew 22 that we discussed in the last chapter—'Love the Lord your God ... love your neighbour as yourself'—some have drawn the conclusion that we are commanded to love ourselves. Three relationships are definitely referred to in that pasage: one with God, one with the neighbour, and one with self. But there are only two commands: love God, and love your neighbour.

There is a grain of truth in the statement, 'You cannot love another till you love yourself', though that grain of truth is probably not recognized by the proponents of this view. The truth is, God provides the only measure of the worth of a man or woman; anything else is wrong and therefore forms a wrong basis of respect. The humanistic society in which we live has developed a multitude of scales for measuring the worth of a person and most of us are led to believe at an early age that we must compete on one or more of these scales for the respect of our peers and our own self-respect. Since we are evaluating ourselves, and other people by erroneous standards, we find we have problems developing respect, for ourselves or anyone else. Paul and

Sandy Cork reported a 50% improvement in their marriage relationship, and they based most of that on what they learned through the self-concept talk. With hindsight, they were able to see that their biggest problem was that they just had not respected each other or themselves, because they had been using the wrong measuring device. There are many measuring devices, as we have said. Some of the most popular ones are physical attractiveness, intelligence, earning power, social skills, and particular talents, such as art, music, etc; but since none of these are God's measure of the value of a human being none of them accurately records someone's true worth. Some people seem to get along fairly well in the area of self-esteem because they have managed to assign to themselves a scale that is favourable to them, but in actuality, they still have a self-image problem because they have made a false assessment.

A poor self-image also causes relationship problems because it makes us very defensive. Deep, effective relationships are based on open, honest vulnerability. And if I do not think the little person down inside me is honestly worth knowing, I will be afraid to let you know him. This fact alone should be enough to force us to come to grips with who we are in Christ.

There is a fair amount of confusion in Christian circles on this whole issue of a self-image. One of the problem areas is 'the worm mentality'. Some hark back to the hymn, 'Would He devote that sacred head for such a worm as me?' There are always bound to be problems when we get our theology from a hymn book. However, two biblical passages would seem at first sight to reinforce this line of thinking. One of them is Psalm 22:6 which is generally accepted to be a prophetic reference to the Lord on the cross saying, as he bore our sins, 'But I am a worm and not a man, scorned by men and despised by the people.' But it is interesting to note here that there is a comparison between a worm and a man, as though a man were a noble creature and a worm ignoble. This is a comparison between man as God intended man to be, created in his image, and man steeped in sin, fallen and twisted. The Lord Jesus felt like a worm, and not a man, as he bore our sins.

Or we can take Bildad the Shuhite's assessment of man from Job 25:6, 'How much less man, who is but a maggot—a son of man, who is only a worm.' But this is a man's comparison of man compared to God; there is no basis for assuming that God intends us to view ourselves in this way. On the contrary, in Christ God views us as men and women, not worms, because in Christ the very sin that made the Lord Jesus feel like a worm and not a man, has been lifted from us. In Romans 7, Paul is dealing with a battle between his old nature and his new nature. In verses 16–17 he says, 'And if I do what I do not want to do, I agree that the law is good. As it is, it is no longer I myself who do it, but it is sin living in me.' And again in verse 20 he says, 'Now if I do what I do not want to do, it is no longer I who do it, but it is sin living in me that does it.' From this we see a principle that victorious Christian living is not attained by identifying with the old nature, but identifying with the new nature. Paul saw a battle going on within him, two totally different natures, but he identified with the new nature and not the old.

The people who promote the 'worm mentality' are well meaning because they want to make sure that we do not forget our worthlessness outside Christ. However, at the same time they have unwittingly promoted the idea that we should identify with the old nature, rather than the new. But if God had wanted worms he would have started a worm farm.

Three models of self-awareness are given in the Bible: superiority, inferiority and humility.

Superiority and inferiority are based on a wrong foundation. But the life of Moses illustrates all three.

We get quite a bit of insight from Stephen's speech before the Sanhedrin in Acts 7.

At that time Moses was born, and he was no ordinary child. For three months he was cared for in his father's house. When he was placed outside, Pharaoh's daughter brought him up and raised him as her own son. Moses was educated in all the wisdom of the Egyptians and was powerful in speech and action.

When Moses was forty years old, he decided to visit his fellow Israelites. He saw one of them being ill-treated by an Egyptian, so he went to his defence and avenged him by killing the Egyptian. Moses thought that his own people would realize that God was using him to rescue them, but they did not. The next day Moses came upon two Israelites who were fighting. He tried to reconcile them by saying, 'Men, you are brothers, why do you want to hurt each other?'

But the man who was ill-treating the other pushed Moses aside and said, 'Who made you ruler and judge over us? Do you want to kill me as you killed the Egyptian yesterday?' When Moses heard this, he fled to Midian, where he settled as a foreigner and had two sons. (Acts 7:20–29)

We see some very interesting things here. First, that Moses was educated with all the wisdom of the Egyptians. Education may have been one of his measuring scales. It gave him the confidence to be 'powerful in speech and action'. It is also very evident that Moses considered himself the 'natural' choice to lead Israel out of captivity. After all, had he not taken all the management and leadership training courses that the Egyptians had to offer? And were not his own people simply makers of bricks and gatherers of straw, who had been deprived of an education for four hundred years? Surely, by any human measuring device you might want to use, he would be the logical choice. Certainly, when he killed the Egyptian, they must recognize that as guerilla activity. But they did not, and they were not able to get into his office and see all his diplomas hanging on the wall, and they did not recognize his qualifications, either. The measuring scale he was using had no value with them, and he was toppled from superiority into a tailspin of inferiority. So he fled and grovelled in inferiority for forty years on the other side of a mountain.

Then one day Moses met God in a burning bush. God was to commission Moses to do the very thing he had attempted to do forty years before in his own strength. However, as we listen to the dialogue between God and Moses, we get the idea that God was having no easy time convincing Moses. Moses was anything but confident. In Exodus 3:13 he says, 'Suppose I go to the Israelites and say to them, "The God of your fathers has sent me to you," and they ask me, "What is his name?" Then what shall I tell them?'

In verse 14 we read that God replied to Moses, 'I AM WHO I AM. This is what you are to say to the Israelites: "I AM has sent me to you."' God went on to assure him that, 'The elders of Israel will listen to you.... But I know the King of Egypt will not let you go unless a mighty hand compels him.... So I will stretch out my hand and strike the Egyptians with all the wonders that I will perform among them. After that he will let you go' (verses 18–20).

So God promised him, but Moses was not convinced. Exodus 4:1: 'What if they do not believe me or listen to me, and say, "The Lord did not appear to you"?' Therefore God gave him three small miracles: a staff that would turn into a snake and then back into a staff; the ability to put his hand into his cloak and withdraw it covered with leprosy and to repeat the process and have it healed; and also the ability to tip water out of the River Nile and have it turn to blood on the ground.

But Moses was still not satisfied. In verse 10 he said, 'Oh Lord, I have never been eloquent, neither in the past nor since you have spoken to your servant. I am slow of speech and tongue' (which is not what Stephen said about him!).

In verse 11, the Lord said to him, 'Who gave man his mouth? Who makes him deaf or mute? Who gives him sight or makes him blind? Is it not I, the Lord? Now go; I will help you speak and will teach you what to say.'

But in verse 13 we read that Moses still protested: 'Oh

Lord, please send someone else to do it.' He was really trying God's patience.

Verse 14 says that the Lord's anger 'burned against Moses'. God said, 'What about your brother, Aaron, the Levite? I know he can speak well. He is already on his way to meet you, and his heart will be glad when he sees you. You shall speak to him and put words in his mouth; I will help both of you speak and will teach you what to do. He will speak to the people for you, and it will be as if he were your mouth and as if you were God to him' (verses 14–16). God was angry with Moses because his inferiority complex had caused God to have to hire two men to do the job of one.

As we read on and on about this, we see that clear over into the last verse of chapter 6 Moses was still not on a good footing: 'But Moses said to the Lord, "Since I speak with faltering lips, why would Pharaoh listen to me?"'

Chapter 7 begins: 'The Lord said to Moses, "See, I have made you like God to Pharaoh, and your brother Aaron will be your prophet."'

It seems highly possible that, at that point, Moses at last got the vision. The penny finally dropped that all God was doing was asking Moses to make himself available for God to work through him. What was important was not Moses' qualifications or lack of qualifications, but the fact that God was going to be operating through him to such a degree that Pharaoh would think Moses was God and that Aaron was his prophet. Moses had gone from superiority (depending on his own high assessment of himself by human standards) to inferiority (depending on his low human assessment); but God had brought him to a state of humility. Humility is the ability to assess oneself accurately and to recognize that God will make up the deficits. Because of his new state of humility, Moses was able to step out of inferiority and go on to be the greatest leader the world had ever known.

Major Ian Thomas in his book *The Saving Life of Christ* (Zondervan) has a chapter titled 'Any Old Bush Will Do'. In it, he has an imaginary dialogue between God and

43

Moses at the burning bush.

> Moses, you have done a wise thing in making intelligent inquiry, for you thought that this was a very remarkable bush. You thought that there must be something about it at once peculiar and wonderful, something unique, that it could burn and burn and burn, and go on burning, and yet not burn itself out. But you are wrong—you are *quite* wrong! Do you see that bush over there? That scruffy, scraggy looking thing—*that* bush would have done! Do you see this beautiful looking bush, so shapely and fine—*this* bush would have done! For you see, Moses, *any old bush* will do—*any* old bush—if only *God* is in the bush! The trouble with you, Moses, is this: forty years ago, learned in all the wisdom of the Egyptians, mighty in word and deed, you admired your own foliage! You thought you were some bush! But you burned yourself out in 24 hours, and you have been a heap of ashes for forty years! If this bush that you have admired were depending upon its own substance to sustain the flame, it too would burn itself out in 24 hours; it too would be a heap of ashes like you. But it is not the *bush* that sustains the flame, it is God *in* the bush; and *any old bush* will do!

The Bible refers to a godly self-concept in three ways: humility, a sober judgement and a self-love. Humility: 'God opposes the proud but gives grace to the humble' (1 Peter 5:5). Sober judgement, which one might call an accurate self-appraisal, is in Romans 12:3: 'For by the grace given me I say to every one of you: Do not think of yourself more highly than you ought, but rather think of yourself with sober judgement, in accordance with the measure of faith God has given you.' And then there is self-love, as in 'Love your neighbour as yourself' (Matt 22:39). Because many psychologists have taken this self-love concept into a humanistic dimension, many Christians prefer to avoid it altogether lest they be confused with the psychologists. But the term appears in the Bible far too many times to be ignored. However, each time it appears it is always *agape* love.

To come to grips with the biblical meaning of self-love, it is necessary to look at the biblical meaning of love. As we have seen in chapter 2, to love another person with *agape* love means to invest your resources in their wellbeing; to do the right thing to meet their need even when your emotions tell you otherwise. To love yourself, then, means to be committed to the same potential in your own life that God is, and to put into your own life whatever is required to make you an effective tool in God's hands. Hence Proverbs 19:8 states, 'He who gets wisdom loves his own soul.' Consequently, self-love is not so much an opinion as right actions based on sober judgement. Possibly a less confusing term might be self-stewardship.

The word 'humility', unfortunately, carries a lot of 'psychological baggage' that tends to distort its meaning. We somehow associate humility with inferiority, thinking that to be humbled is to be made to feel inferior. To some degree we tend to associate humility with grovelling in inferiority, as with Moses at the burning bush. However, the Lord Jesus was humble, and one cannot imagine him grovelling. Humility is simply recognizing, as Moses eventually did, that I cannot—but God *can*. It is realizing that because God is the working force in my life, I can do anything that he calls me to do. Consequently, we conclude that humility is the biblical term for a healthy self-concept.

Our natural tendency is to try to overcome feelings of inferiority by striving for superiority. But superiority presupposes competition, and God has addressed this compare-compete-and-conquer mentality in 2 Corinthians 10:12: 'We do not dare to classify or compare ourselves with some who commend themselves. When they measure themselves by themselves and compare themselves with themselves, they are not wise.' Even if for no other reason, they are not wise because comparing yourself to someone else is like trying to add together apples and oranges. We are all unique individuals with specific purposes in God's economy.

Genesis 4:6–7 gives us a biblical basis for feeling good

about ourselves. After Cain's offering was rejected by the Lord, the Lord said to Cain, 'Why are you angry? Why is your face downcast? If you do what is right, will you not be accepted?' In other words, if you do right, you feel right and that's all right by God. According to the Bible, the way to have right feelings towards ourselves is by obeying God. However, the fact that we are mere mortals means that we all have bouts of disobedience. On the other hand, Ephesians 2:10 tells us that we are God's workmanship in Christ and therefore we are of worth to him. It also shows that he has a plan for our significance as we do 'the good works which he has already prepared for us to do'.

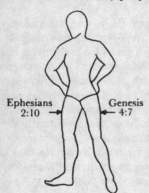

Ephesians 2:10

Genesis 4:7

In the illustration, we are demonstrating that our own particular feelings of self-worth must be supported on two legs. One is the Genesis 4 leg. This says that if we do right we will feel right. The other is the Ephesians 2:10 leg, which speaks of God's opinion of us. You will notice that most of the weight, however, is on the Ephesians 2:10 leg. The reason for this is that the Genesis 4:7 leg frequently gets knocked out from under us. If our self-worth were based only on how well we were obeying God, or how well we were performing, we would often fall flat on our face, and even worse, might not have the courage to get to our feet again.

David was a man after God's own heart, not because he was continually obedient, but because he got back up again after his disobedience. If we are unaware of our basic worth in God's eyes, we can be easily demoralized by the adversary, who will continually tell us that our failures are a reason for not going on with God. A second problem that arises when obedience is a criterion for self-worth, is that sometimes what we regard as obedience is really only behaviour that conforms to our own Christian sub-culture. Consequently, if that leg is the one on which we are placing most of our weight, we will not have the ability to become non-conformists when we begin to sense that something is radically wrong in the behaviour of our own group. What has actually happened is that we have slipped on to a new scale of measurement, developed by our Christian sub-culture, and we are now competing on this new scale. We are very vulnerable to the feedback that we get from those around us. So our self-image is now based not only on how we think we are doing, but on how others think we are doing—which actually means how we think they think we are doing. This is obviously very precarious. It also seems to be exactly the trap that King Saul fell into.

The Bible tells us that Saul was a head taller than any man in Israel; but he had a self-image problem. In fact, on his coronation day they could not find him, and when eventually they did, he was hiding among the baggage. Later on, the prophet Samuel came to Saul with instructions from the Lord: 'Now go, attack the Amalekites and totally destroy everything that belongs to them. Do not spare them; put to death men and women, children and infants, cattle and sheep, camels and donkeys' (1 Sam 15:3).

So Saul and his army took off on this mission. 'But Saul and the army spared Agag [the king of the Amalekites] and the best of the sheep and cattle, the fat calves and lambs—everything that was good' (verse 9).

Then Samuel went out to visit the camp. Saul greeted him somewhat like a child who has been caught with his hand in the biscuit barrel:

> The Lord bless you! I have carried out the Lord's instructions.
> But Samuel said, 'What then is this bleating of sheep in my ears? What is this lowing of cattle I hear?'
> Saul answered, 'The soldiers brought them from the

Amalekites; they spared the best of the sheep and cattle to sacrifice to the Lord your God, but we totally destroyed the rest.'

Samuel said, 'Although you were once small in your own eyes [and remember, he was a head taller than anyone else in Israel], did you not become the head of the tribes of Israel? The Lord anointed you king over Israel. And sent you on a mission, saying, 'Go and completely destroy those wicked people, the Amalekites; make war on them until you have wiped them out.' Why did you not obey the Lord? (verses 15, 17–19a)

Knowing what we do about Saul, it is not hard to read between the lines and see the probable dynamics of the situation. First, from a material perspective, it does not seem very bright simply to waste a lot of prime livestock. And Saul was probably getting feedback to this effect from some of his officers. And then he may have heard a comment from someone along the lines of: 'I wonder who's running this country, Saul or Samuel?' A remark like that might have been just enough to push him over the edge. The answer to the question, 'Why did you not obey the Lord?' comes in 1 Samuel 15:24: 'I was afraid of the people and so I gave in to them.' I do not think the Bible depicts Saul as any more disobedient than David. But it is reasonable to assume that David stood on two legs—and Saul on one.

Our subconscious operates a lot like a computer. That is, it files away every bit of data without necessarily making a judgement as to whether it is right or wrong. A lot of the material that is filed away is just plain rubbish. Our conscious mind is smart enough to avoid most of this when making intelligent decisions because it is able to judge the accuracy of the material. However, this flotsam and jetsam that is hanging around in our minds is the material from which attitudes are made up.

I think this can best be demonstrated if we talk about prejudices. I (Dave) was brought up in a home where respect for all was taught. Unfortunately, I had a grand-father who was an exact copy of Alf Garnett, or his American counterpart, Archie Bunker. He treated my grandmother just as Alf Garnett treated his wife. And she responded like Alf Garnett's wife. My grandfather was the most bigoted individual I have ever met. He seemed to revel in his vocabulary of uncomplimentary names for minority groups. Most of all, he delighted in ridiculing Jews. I can remember once coming home from Sunday school and asking my mother if Granddaddy realized that Jesus was a Jew. Quite frankly, I had a hard time reconciling the two views. In Sunday school they were telling me how wonderful Jesus was, and my grandfather was telling me how terrible Jews were.

Well, naturally, now that I am a Christian, I see the Jews as a special people and I feel a special excitement for Hebrew Christians. And quite naturally I tend to view activities in the Middle East as though the Jews are the 'good guys' and all the rest are 'baddies'. But still, somehow, when I get in a financial transaction with someone who is Jewish, something deep down inside says, 'Watch it, he's smarter than you are.' Obviously this is old data coming up that my grandfather programmed into my computer for me. It is not limited to Jews. I find that I continually have to make intelligent decisions to disregard trash that is in my computer.

That same programming goes on with regard to our worth as a person. I once knew a pastor whose name was Ed. He told us that as a teenager, whenever he worked with his dad, he was bombarded with comments like, 'There's something wrong with your head, Ed', 'Ed, use your head', 'Ed, you'll never get on'. He told us that he spent the first twenty years of his ministry trying to build the biggest church in town just to prove to his dad that his head was all right. The fact is that most of us have had a lifetime of faulty computer programming. We have remarks filed away to the effect that our nose is too big, our ears stick out too far, our Adam's apple is too prominent, we are not responsible, not dependable, etc. This is not material that we usually take conscious cognizance of, because it rides below the surface, more like an emotion than a thought process. However, God was very aware that this would happen. I am quite sure this is why we have the admonition in Philippians 4:8: 'Finally, brothers, whatever is true, whatever is noble, whatever is right, whatever is pure, whatever is lovely, whatever is admirable—if anything is excellent or praiseworthy—think about such things.' We are only to think about what is true and right. And comments like, 'Is that your nose, or are you eating a banana?' do not fall into that category. And even our failures, however true they may be, are not the things we are to dwell on, it is whatever is noble, whatever is admirable, things that are excellent, things that are praiseworthy.

In the last paragraph we mentioned not dwelling on failures, but this needs to be qualified. First, there needs to be a distinction between behaviour and performance. Behaviour has to do with character, which is a direct reflection of our walk with God. When we feel bad because of poor behaviour, that is not to be glossed over, because it is the conviction of the Holy Spirit. However, once we have put it right through confession, we are not to dwell on it. Performance has to do with our abilities. We should not dwell on these any longer than it takes to determine steps for future improvement. 'If we confess our sins, he is faithful and just and will forgive us our sins and purify us from all unrighteousness' (1 Jn 1:9).

People who feel inferior because of poor behaviour need to memorize this verse and to meditate on two concepts. First, we must confess sin and assume responsibility for our actions. Second, we must accept it as a fact that once our sin is confessed, we are cleansed from all unrighteousness.

In performance, we may need to seek forgiveness from God for failure in two areas. One is where behaviour and performance merge, as with laziness or unethical shortcuts. The second is where we assess our worth as persons by how well we can perform certain tasks.

We must judge our behaviour by God's standards. Some performance *can* be measured by human standards but some like the effectiveness of our witness, can only be determined from an eternal perspective. However, our overall worth as people can only be measured by God.

Well, we have stated the problem: faulty programming. The only way that we know to overcome faulty programming, is to develop a new program that is in touch with the facts. The solution lies in understanding how God views us. But before that, it might be worth entering into our program how we view God.

God is sovereign. He is very much in control, very much aware of the most minute details. 'Are not two sparrows sold for a penny? Yet not one of them will fall to the ground apart from the will of your Father. And even the very hairs of our head are all numbered' (Matt 10:29–30).

He is a God of integrity. 'God is not a man, that he should lie, nor a son of man, that he should change his mind. Does he speak and then not act? Does he promise and not fulfil?' (Num 23:19).

God has a definite purpose for this world and everything that is in it. 'For the Lord Almighty has purposed, and who can thwart him? His hand is stretched out, and who can turn it back?' (Isaiah 14:27).

His purpose concerns me. '"For I know the plans I have for you," declares the Lord, "plans to prosper you and not to harm you, plans to give you hope and a future"' (Jer 29:11). The Good News Bible renders this: 'plans to bring about the future you hope for.' When this verse says that God would bring about the future that the people had hoped for, it is stating that God is interested in the happiness of his people—as Psalms 37:4 says: 'Delight yourself in the Lord and he will give you the desires of your heart' (Ps 37:4). Whether that means he will give the present desires that we have in our heart, or will change our desires to match his ultimate will, it still tells us that, at the bottom line, if we are delighting in the Lord, our desires will ultimately be fulfilled in our life and ultimate fulfilment in our lives will coincide.

How does the sovereign God of integrity, purpose and compassion view me? He sees me as made in his image, fallen and twisted but redeemed for the purpose of a relationship with him that he desires. For this reason he says, 'I, even I, am he who blots out your transgressions, for my own sake, and remembers your sins no more' (Is 43:25). Most of us are well aware that God has to blot our sins for our sake, but we do not often think about the fact that he blotted out our sins for his sake, because he desired a relationship with us, and the only way he could have a relationship was to blot out our sins.

Although I am a sinner, he sees me as forgiven. 'He forgave us all our sins, having cancelled the written code, with its regulations, that was against us and that stood opposed to us; he took it away, nailing it to the cross' (Col 2:13b–14). Not only am I forgiven, but much more, I am adopted. 'In love he predestined us to be adopted as his sons through Jesus Christ, in accordance with his pleasure and will' (Eph 1:5). And even more: this sovereign God, creator of the universe, by his Spirit dwells in me. 'I will ask the Father, and he will give you another Counsellor to be with you for ever—the Spirit of truth. The world cannot accept him, because it neither sees him nor knows him. But you know him, for he lives with you and will be in you' (Jn 14:16–17).

And as if all that were not enough, God already has a ministry laid out for me to do. 'For we are God's workmanship, created in Christ Jesus to do good works, which God prepared in advance for us to do' (Eph 2:10).

Consider again the Good News version of Jeremiah 29:11: 'I alone know the plans that I have for you, plans to bring you prosperity and not disaster, plans to bring about the future you hope for.' We begin to realize that this is possible as we grow in the Christian life, because the more we walk with God and understand his thoughts, the more we hope

God's hopes. God has hopes for our life. This is why it is so important that we program our computer with the facts. We highly recommend memorizing these verses so that they can be appropriately filed away. When the adversary pushes the hopeless button, we can immediately reach over and push the hope button.

C. S. Lewis gives a definition of faith in *Mere Christianity*. He says, 'Faith is the art of holding on to things our reason has once accepted, in spite of our changing mood.' In other words, the only way we can win over emotions is with a firm grasp of the facts.

Psychologists tell us we have a need for love and significance. These needs are already met in Christ. I am loved by the greatest source of love in the universe. 'This is how we know what love is: Jesus Christ laid down his life for us' (1 John 3:16a). And I certainly have significance. God has called me to be a functioning part of the body and to bear fruit in his ministry. 'I no longer call you servants, because a servant does not know his master's business. Instead, I have called you friends, for everything that I learned from my Father I have made known to you. You did not choose me, but I chose you and appointed you to go and bear fruit—fruit that will last' (Jn 15:15–16a).

This significance does not have to be judged by our standing within the Christian community, but by our faithfulness to God. We do not have the ability to judge the eternal significance of specific accomplishments within the kingdom of God—but God does.

Some psychologists say that our self-esteem has three parts—belonging, worth and competence. These, too, are all met by God. I belong to the Father: 'How great is the love the Father has lavished on us, that we should be called the children of God! And that is what we are! The reason the world does not know us is that it did not know him' (1 Jn 3:1) Joyce and I were abandoned by our fathers as children. We both know that we have a heavenly Father who will never abandon us.

53

We also have worth: 'For you know that it was not with perishable things such as silver or gold that you were redeemed from the empty way of life handed down to you from your forefathers, but with the precious blood of Jesus Christ, a lamb without blemish or defect' (1 Pet 1:18–19). That certainly gives me an imparted value greater than the crown jewels, or all the silver and gold in the world, the precious blood of Jesus Christ.

Confidence? 'I can do everything through him who gives me strength' (Phil 4:13). God will provide everything I need for each thing he calls me to do. One of the most important aspects of understanding that all our needs are met in Christ, concerns our relationships. We can be freed from manipulating people around us into meeting our needs, and we are able to minister to theirs. A person who is well aware of who he is in Christ, is thus equipped to serve others. The classic example of this is the life of Christ.

> Jesus knew that the Father had put all things under his power, and that he had come from God and was returning to God; so he got up from the meal, took off his outer clothing, and wrapped a towel round his waist. After that, he poured water into a basin and began to wash his disciples' feet, drying them with the towel that was wrapped around him (Jn 13:3–5).

Here is a statement of Jesus' self-awareness—he knew the Father had put all things under his power, that he came from God and that he was returning to God—followed by an example of extreme servanthood. It is significant that this very menial task chosen by Jesus, in a specific teaching situation, was preceded by this very rare statement of self-awareness. There is another statement similar to this in Philippians 2:6–7: 'Who, being in very nature God, did not consider equality with God something to be grasped, but made himself nothing, taking the very nature of a servant, being made in human likeness.' In both instances, the statement of self-awareness is followed by servanthood. A person who knows who he is does not really care what other people think of his status. He is freed to serve. Jesus washed his disciples' feet to teach them this lesson.

'Do you understand what I have done for you?' he asked them. 'You call me "Teacher" and "Lord", and rightly so, for that is what I am. Now that I, your Lord and Teacher, have washed your feet, you also should wash one another's feet. I have set you an example that you should do as I have done for you. I tell you the truth, no servant is greater than his master, nor is a messenger greater than the one who sent him' (Jn 13:12–16).

Jesus was not self-centred; he was God-centred. Because God so loved the world and Jesus was God-centred, he naturally was other-oriented. Secular answers to self-image problems are by nature man-centred and therefore relative to other men and man's idea of success or failure. Thus, the more we are influenced by humanism, the more self-centred we become. The more self-centred we become, the more we find ourselves comparing ourselves with others. And we are on a treadmill of competition with others, judging our worth against standards that have no relation to true worth. We cannot serve other people because we have not got enough energy left over from the competition.

Conversely, the more we seek a God-centred approach to life, the less self-centred we become. Then we find that we almost automatically become other-oriented. We love and want to serve those whom God dwelling within us loves.

The fact of it is that most of us have not become great in God's kingdom because we have not become servants.

And we have not become servants because we are trying so hard to become great.

For further consideration

1. In what way does low self-image affect our marriage?
2. Discuss the relationship between self-respect and respecting others.

3. In what areas do I have a tendency to have a 'critical spirit' and what does this tell me about myself?

Chapter 4

Tuning Your Trumpet

In September 1983 we started on a new phase in our life and ministry. Community living. We moved into Beck House with Joe and Brenda Hickok, who are in charge of one phase of our ministry, and four other single adults. When our next door neighbour heard what we were about to do, she said, 'My, you'll have to learn to be quiet about a lot of things', and she was a bit surprised when we told her, 'No, we'll have to do a lot more talking.' When you have two people living in a house, you have one relationship. When you have eight people living in a house, you have fifty-six relationships; and relationships take communication, not to mention the fact that a lot of basic understanding is necessary in order for eight people to live together and function reasonably well. There must be an understanding about who is going to mow the lawn, chop the wood, do the washing up, wash and iron the clothes, do the typing, etc. Then there are little idiosyncrasies that require special policy-making, like, 'Please do not soften the butter in the microwave, and chop firewood outdoors, not indoors.'

One Air Force major who attended a Marriage Weekend held a Master's degree in a related field. He said that he was amazed that one could teach communication from the Bible. The Bible does not exactly read like a communication manual, but it *is* communication and it speaks of communication; it is a record of communication. It also gives us certain life-principles, such as, 'speaking the truth in love', which must be reflected in our communication (Eph 4:15).

Someone has said that at the bottom of every problem in the world there is a communication problem. That might be stretching it, but we would be willing to go out on a limb and say that at the bottom of every marital difficulty, there is a communication problem. Paul says, 'For if the trumpet gives an uncertain sound, who shall prepare himself for the battle?' (1 Cor 14:8, AV). Needs and expectations go unmet because of inept communication by people who will then go on to accuse their partners of being insensitive.

Marriage Weekends, as well as this book, place a great deal of emphasis on communication. This emphasis, however, should not be so much on specific methods or gimmicks, but on the priority of communication throughout our relationship. The process of maturity itself involves a constant reassessment of our ability to communicate, and a continual upgrading of the priority of communication in our life, both speaking and listening. Amos 3:3 says, 'Do two walk together unless they have agreed to do so?' They must agree on the destination and they must also agree on the route they will travel to reach that destination. The song says, 'O ye'll tak' the high road, and I'll tak' the low road, and I'll be in Scotland afore ye': two people are going to the same destination, but are not walking together. Too few courting couples talk about goals for their marriage, let alone ways for achieving those goals. And everyone is aware that there are day by day adjustments on the course that must be communicated as well.

There is more that needs to be communicated than goals and objectives and who empties the rubbish bin. People who have studied communication make numerous distinctions between the types and levels of communication in which people get involved. There are many ways to divide this up. We have chosen three levels in order to illustrate differing levels of communication: cliché; facts and opinions; and feeling level communication.

Cliché: this is bus-stop conversation. It really is nothing more than a polite acknowledgement of the other person's presence. Most of us do not even think when we do this. One morning we were at the hospital; Joyce was having a thyroid scan because a lump had suddenly appeared on her throat, and I was there because they had noticed a spot on my last x-ray and they wanted to shoot more pictures from a differing angle. Twice during this rather trying visit, when old friends ran into us in the hallway, we were asked, 'How are you?' and we just automatically replied, 'Fine, how are you?' Once the cliché-level conversation was over, we went on to tell them why we were there (everything turned out fine, by the way!).

Facts and opinions: this includes everything from comments on the weather, to where we are taking our holiday, to politics, and on to abstract points of theology. It may be intellectual, but it is not very personal. To talk about the weather and holidays is fairly safe; our opinions and ideas may be unique, and may even get us into trouble on occasions, but none of this is real relationship communication.

Feeling level communication: this is gut-level communication, real relationship communication, because it goes beyond the intellectual and into the uniquely personal part of our being.

Naturally, some facts that are communicated are very personal, and these facts usually have an important place in relationships because they are given so that we can know each other better. But they are generally given in conjunction with a feeling. Take, for example, the woman who decided in a counselling session that it was high time that she told us, as well as her husband, that her father had molested her when she was fourteen years old. This was a fact, not a feeling; but it was a fact given to explain a feeling, and it was a very important piece of information in dealing with their situation.

Feelings are the result of a lifetime of experiences. They make us unique and cause different people to react differently in different situations. We do not always react openly, though, because we assume our feelings are not acceptable. Sharing such feelings can be like giving a special present to our partner, because it lets them know that we are willing to trust them with something that society may have already taught us is unacceptable. We may fear things that we think Christians should not fear, or have likes or dislikes that we think we should not have, or that nobody will understand. We ought to be the kind of partners who will try to understand, and even if we do not, will always accept.

Being open and honest, sharing all that we are, is a part of the New Testament principle of vulnerability. The God of the Old Testament who spoke in the fire and smoke and rumbling mountains became vulnerable to the point of walking dusty roads, washing feet and admonishing his followers to do likewise. The gospel was not communicated from a position of superiority or safety, but from the point of vulnerability; and so is the Christian life.

The word 'vulnerable' implies a risk, the possibility that a price may have to be paid. It also implies trust. We are most attracted to those who trust us. Naturally, we make ourselves more attractive to our partners when we trust them. There is no relationship without trust, and no trust without vulnerability. Charles and Susan were experiencing many conflicts in their marriage. On the Marriage Weekend, they recognized that it was mainly because, to some degree, they were expecting conflicts; he, especially, always had his guard up. The last thing he wanted to do was to become vulnerable. Over the course of the Weekend, they realized that this was a missing ingredient in their marriage. He made a commitment to God to be as open as God would give him the strength to be, which was reciprocated by Susan. Six months later, they claimed a 100% improvement in their marriage, and gave most of the credit to their commitment to be vulnerable with each other.

There are some very important principles in sharing feelings. First, and very obvious, if we want to encourage our partners to share on a feeling level, we must not condemn the feelings. Right or wrong, they feel the way they do under those circumstances. We may be able to ease our partner out of, say, anxious feelings by very understandingly and lovingly working through the situation over a period of time, but we must not dare attempt to do it by making fun of them.

Secondly, our feelings may be triggered off by our partner, but they cannot be blamed on our partner. It takes a lifetime of experiences to develop feelings; circumstances can only arouse what is already present. For instance, when our children were growing up, we lived in Florida, and the children often went barefoot. Our youngest son, however, loved to walk around in his stockinged feet. This was unacceptable; it wears them out too quickly and gets them far too dirty, so I found myself saying, 'Billy, take your socks off or put your shoes on.' Five minutes later: 'Billy, take your socks off or put your shoes on.' Now, Billy was a good kid. He really wanted to please. But at that time I had serious doubts. No one could be that absent-minded. He could see how frustrated it made me. Was he deliberately trying to get back at me for something? Could a ten-year-old have a stocking demon that needed to be cast out? It sounds funny now, and I really ought to be absolutely ashamed to admit how tied up in knots I got over that. I could see him in his stockinged feet and just about go 'ballistic'. But other people could look at his stockinged feet, and it did not bother them in the least, so there is no way I could blame the way I felt on a ten-year-old child. I had to blame it on the way I was dealing with the problem.

Feeling level dialogue is not a place to argue, make decisions, place responsibility, solve problems, or plan the future. It is a place to learn about each other, to know and be known. None of this is to say that wrong feelings are to be condoned, but criticism is not the most effective tool in dealing with them, and therefore it is out of place in feeling level communication. We will seldom talk on the feeling level if we feel this will result in criticism, although we know that if we do share our feelings, we are opening ourselves to the possibility of being criticized. This vulnerability must be honoured if there is to be continued vulnerability.

Some people say, 'Feelings are neutral things. There is nothing right or wrong about them, they are just feelings. They exist and must be faced. It is not the emotion that is the sin, but it is how you act on it.' This notion is certainly true, but is somewhat limited. It is true with an emotion like anger. The Bible tells us that God was angry; it tells us that we can be angry but must not sin. Anger is a God-given emotion, probably serving as a catalyst to produce immediacy in resolving relationship difficulties. If we never got angry, we probably never would take a lot of the action we do take—even the right actions. What do we do with this energy? Do we blow up, clam up, or direct it towards the problem? Naturally, we should direct it towards the problem, not the person.

On the other hand, if you hate your children or your mother-in-law, that, in itself, meets the biblical criteria of sin. But even obvious sin seldom needs to be pointed out in deep sharing. The person sharing usually is very aware of this already. Careful listening and probing questions may well bring enough facts to light to point out an obvious solution. It is a pretty good rule of thumb in a sharing situation like this not to give advice unless you are asked for it. One can get counsel from a friend, and one can be a friend with a counsellor, but there is a distinction between friends and counsellors, and sometimes we need friends but not counsellors. Husbands and wives need to know how to be that kind of a friend. Negative feelings are sometimes to the mind what a headache is to the body, an indication that something is wrong. Frequently an aspirin is all that is required to get rid of a headache, and talking can soothe an emotional pain. But there are occasions when, as with aspirins, simply airing a problem is too superficial, and some deep reassurance between partners is necessary.

Feeling level conversations do not have to be scheduled. Consider Mike and Diana, who have a twelve-year-old retarded boy. Paul is, at best, exasperating. He is noisy, uncooperative and hyper-active. Mike is a very easy-going person who could probably tolerate a disco in his lounge while reading his evening paper. Diana's temperament is a bit more exacting, which means that Paul gets on her nerves much more quickly than he does with Mike. She does not hate Paul, but frequently talks as though she does. This does not go unnoticed by Mike, who is more concerned about a less-than-admirable quality in his wife, than with its effect on Paul. He would say, 'You're getting all vinegary again', or 'Aren't you being a bit sharpish, love?' In the past, this approach brought temporary relief, except for the time when she bellowed out, 'So would you if you had to be home all day!' But one day, after some particularly unedifying comments, he thought, 'Attacking her response to Paul always seems to wind up as an attack on Diana. I love her, and I want to meet her needs.' He met her at the bedroom door after getting Paul down for the night, put his arm around her and said, 'He's really getting to you, isn't he?' This uncorked an avalanche of feeling level dialogue, where she was able to pour out her frustrations and deal with her attitude problem. They had a chance to pray about it, whereupon *she* asked *him* to remind her each time her voice got sharp. That in itself did not solve the problem, but the reminders given after that pointed back to a time of deep

fact   faith   feeling

sharing and new commitment, rather than to a long record of comments from a critical husband.

Campus Crusade for Christ has this little train in their book, *Knowing God Personally*. It says,

> A train is pulled by the engine and not the guard's van. In the same way, put your trust in the facts of God's trustworthiness and His promises. The more fuel of faith that is put onto these facts of God's promises, the more his power will be released in your life. Don't allow faith to depend on your feelings.

This is certainly sound advice, but sometimes, when we talk about feeling level communication, we find people's minds doing a cross-reference between what we are saying about the importance of sharing feelings and what is said in the context of this diagram regarding our faith. These are not conflicting views at all. Acknowledging our feelings and operating on our feelings are two different things. Some points to be remembered are:

Good feelings are generally the result of right actions.

BUT:

Good feelings are not necessary to initiate right actions. We can initiate right actions whether we feel like it or not.

Our feelings frequently tell us that decisions need to be made.

BUT:

Decisions should not be based on our feelings.

'Be quick to listen, slow to speak and slow to become angry' (Js 1:19).

For further consideration

Think of a problem you have had which was the result of *not* communicating. What could be done to help avoid future occurrences?

Consider: Feelings tell us that decisions need to be made. But decisions should never be made on feelings.

Chapter 5

Dealing With Conflict

Someone has said that when two people agree on everything one of them is unnecessary. Differences of opinion are absolutely unavoidable. There will always be a conflict of ideas. This chapter is designed to answer certain questions about conflict.

Why do we have conflicts?

How can conflicts be minimized?

What are the most common methods of dealing with conflict?

How should conflicts be handled?

Why conflicts? We can answer this question from a spiritual perspective by simply going back to Romans 8:29 and remembering that God is in the business of conforming us to the image of Jesus Christ. This is a character-building process which evidently cannot be accomplished by sailing a smooth course. Mariners depend heavily on weather forecasts so that they can avoid storms whenever possible, but this does not relieve them of the responsibility of knowing how to handle their ship in rough weather. Jesus said, 'In this world you will have trouble. But take heart! I have overcome the world' (Jn 16:33). This is a very strong statement which tells us that life's problems—and they usually take the form of interpersonal conflict—are unavoidable.

Jesus goes on to tell us that in him we have the ability to cope. In other words, he does not promise us fair weather, but good seamanship.

The further we remove ourselves from the Christian perspective, the more complex the reasons for conflict become. Immaturity, selfishness, ignorance, stubbornness, poor communication and a host of other factors, complicate the issue. Although we are redeemed, we are redeemed sinners. These manifestations of our old natures do complicate our lives. Most of us have no problem in understanding these complicating factors; the problem arises when we feel that all conflicts are traced back to these factors alone. Consequently, when a conflict does arise in a Christian relationship, or even closer to home, in a Christian marriage, we automatically feel we are failures.

Constant disagreement is not necessarily a hallmark of a healthy relationship, but it is certainly not the greatest danger. The greatest danger would be two people who always thought alike on every issue. However, this is not a danger we need concern ourselves with, because it just does not work out that way in real life. It is our experience that God never puts two people together who think alike on every issue. It is simply not profitable in God's economy to do so. God is interested in relationships that stretch our character. He puts the goal-oriented with the procrastinator and the frivolous with the sober-minded. He matches the irresponsible with the over-responsible, the abrasive with the gentle, and the silly with the sober.

Understanding this concept has in itself brought much hope into the hearts of couples who have been married two or three years and feel they must have made a mistake. Surely they must have missed God's will for their lives! Obviously, they had not prayed enough about choosing a life partner; certainly this match was not made in heaven! From the human perspective, these are very logical conclusions when so much polarity seems to exist in a relationship.

Jack and Jo Boggs are good friends of ours. Jack is the pastor of a local Baptist church. He is absolutely one of the nicest people I have ever met. He is very considerate, sensitive, warm, outgoing, and always seems to have the ability to meet people's needs, whether this takes a few well-chosen words or hours of counselling. I am sure that most of the women in his congregation wish that their husbands were just like Jack. But that is not very realistic. Firstly, because we are all unique individuals: God never intended us to be all alike. And secondly, there are real problems in living with 'nice guys'—I am sure Jo Boggs would say 'Amen!' to that!

Jo is a thoughtful, considerate person, as well. However, she has a decidedly different temperament from her husband. She is very goal-oriented and purposeful. She is much more analytical and discerning, and quite frequently has opinions where he does not. She has a much greater ability to see through those individuals who are simply taking advantage of them, and a much greater desire to *do* something about it. This 'complementary' temperament has quite naturally been the source of conflicts throughout their marriage, in everything from squeezing the toothpaste to raising children, and on to dealing with disgruntled deacons. A few years back, they celebrated their twenty-fifth wedding anniversary with their congregation. As custom would dictate, they shared a few gems of wisdom with those present. I am sure Jack gave some good advice; he always does. He is a good Bible teacher, and he specializes in marriage. But whatever he said did not stick with me as well as Jo's comments, which were simply, 'Marriages are made in heaven—but they are worked out here on earth', and 'Divorce was never an option, it never crossed my mind—murder on a few occasions—but never divorce.'

Dave and Carita were two young people who met each other in our fellowship at the Christian Servicemen's Centre. They were not as young as some, both being nearly thirty when they met. Their temperaments were similar to those of Jack and Jo Boggs, but with more polarity. In fact, when they first started going out together, some people even wondered what the attraction was. Not only their temperaments, but their backgrounds too, were entirely different. They were both university graduates, but the similarity ended there. He was the son of a Lutheran pastor and had been raised up in a loving, God-fearing environment. She, on the other hand, was the daughter of a hard-boiled business executive. She had grown up in a very materialistically oriented family, and her experience level was considerably higher, as she had sampled everything the world had to offer. In fact, when we first met her, she was a total women's libber. Her greatest hang-up about inviting Jesus Christ into her life was that he was a man. It is not unusual for a person with this background, once they are converted, to take Christianity very seriously, and Carita was no exception. When she asked Christ to be her Saviour, she also made him Lord, and she grew in leaps and bounds.

When Dave and Carita began to get serious, they explored every possible Christian avenue for knowledge in the art of marriage. They read all the right books, discussed marriage with any Christian couple they could, and spent hours working on their relationship in a very sensible and honourable way. They had the largest, most beautiful and totally God-honouring wedding we have ever attended, and went off for a wonderful honeymoon.

Short honeymoon! It was not long after they got back the backlash hit them. They looked to us as their spiritual Mum and Dad and knew we were on call if they needed help: and that marriage needed more intensive care than a new heart transplant patient. How could this happen? She was such a young and beautiful, blossoming new creature in Christ, and he was certainly the model gentleman. He was very romantic, very considerate. He brought her more flowers in a month than most women see in a lifetime. He always thought about nice things like soft music and candlelight, and took his shoes off at the door to protect the new carpet; they prayed together, studied the Bible together. It was absolutely impossible to think of anything else they could have done to be better prepared for marriage, or anything else that they could do now to enhance their marriage. Except for two things: first, to recognize their differences, understand that God had made them both unique individuals and then placed them together as a part of a growth process. And second, to communicate about these differences.

The first issue that really catapulted this marriage into catastrophe was a very simple situation involving do-it-yourself skills. Dave was intelligent, considerate, witty, and to all outward appearances had the qualifications of an ideal husband—except one. He was not very clever with his hands. In fact, he felt that when it came to home maintenance skills, he had more thumbs than a mitten factory. Carita wanted new curtain rods putting up, and she wanted a shelf in the pantry, and she quite naturally looked to Dave to accomplish this. After all, could not all men do these sorts of things? Which was exactly the way Dave felt—all *real* men could do these sorts of things; but he could not. He saw it as an attack on his masculinity. There were several logical alternatives. He could have called in a friend, hired someone, or possibly even bought a DIY book. But instead, he chose to procrastinate. Procrastination is never a good alternative, but in this particular instance it was the worst, because Carita had the choleric, goal-oriented personality of her father, and to her, procrastination was the unpardonable sin. Procrastination is not very nice, but it seems to be the besetting sin of 'nice guys'. It is the very thing that will cause a goal-oriented individual to go up the wall.

This was certainly not their only area of difference. Their polarity of temperament manifested itself in many other areas of their relationship, and even reared its ugly head in their sex life. They attended a Marriage Weekend when they had only been married three months. They found that not only was there an effective way to deal with conflicts, like being themselves and talking about their differences, but there were also some precautions that could help them minimize conflicts.

Conflicts can be reduced by means of communication skills. Two very simple procedures can reduce both the quantity and magnitude of conflicts. The first is listening. This will minimize conflict, if for no other reason than that it shows consideration for the other person. Someone has said, 'We can best affirm the worth of another person by paying sincere attention to their words.' Most of us are pretty good talkers, but not very good listeners. Sometimes we make the effort to hear, but we really do not listen: listening is a developed skill. The best way to demonstrate good listening is to give appropriate responses. Proverbs 25:11 states, 'A word aptly spoken is like apples of gold in settings of silver.'

The second communication skill is, therefore, the ability to respond properly. The best response for minimizing conflict is known as an understanding response. This is simply the practice of summarizing and paraphrasing what the other person is saying, with a statement such as, 'Did I understand you to say that Dave and Carita have totally different temperaments?' This is a simple device that does two things: it lets the other person know that we are listening (we have to be listening in order to be able to summarize and paraphrase); and it allows us to negotiate for meaning. For instance, the question, 'Do I understand that you are saying Dave's and Carita's problem was their totally different temperaments?' could be answered, 'No, their problem was their failure to recognize and communicate about their differences.' This helps us to crystallize issues to avoid misunderstanding. Obviously, this will not pre-empt all conflicts, but it will isolate the issues, which will in itself tend to make the conflict less volatile.

The way in which we actually deal with conflict is probably as unique as personality itself. And, whether we recognize it or not, we each develop certain tactics that we feel comfortable with. We feel it helps to examine some of the major categories of conflict tactics, because our style of handling conflict definitely influences the relationships that we are in. We want to look at five major approaches, examine some of the motivation behind them, and see what the repercussions are.

Peaceniks are people who want peace at any price. They are not nearly as interested in the relationship as they are in peace. They are not interested in developing their character or anyone else's character. They will do anything imaginable to extricate themselves from a potentially volatile situation. They will leave the room, avoid conversation, insulate themselves psychologically, or turn up the television. Their favourite phrase is, 'Have it your own way'. Many of them consider this to be a very noble way of dealing with conflict. They sometimes fancy themselves as peacemakers, when in actuality they are not willing to make anything; they are just hoping to find it. In Christian terms, many of them see themselves as 'trusting the Lord' to work out the details. But this makes as much sense as praying, 'Give us this day our daily bread', and then expecting to find it on the doorstep, not realizing that God's idea of giving us our daily bread is to give us a job where we can earn it. The theology here is faulty.

The *Conquerors* are people who equate success in a conflict with words like 'triumph', 'victory' and 'superiority'. They may theologize this by saying that they are 'overcomers'. Like the Peaceniks, they are also less interested in the relationship than they are in their own personal satisfaction; but in this case their satisfaction always comes at the expense of a vanquished opponent. They have some interest in building character—yours, not theirs. There are two major motivating forces behind the Conqueror mentality. One is, of course, insecurity. They see losing an argument as a situation which undermines their credibility as human beings. Consequently, a person who continually finds himself using this mode of dealing with conflicts must ask himself if his self-esteem has a proper basis. Another motivation behind the Conqueror mentality is a perverted sense of entertainment; some people just simply love a good scrap. To them, relationships are developed for the sole purpose of having someone to fight with. And if one thing drives this type of person up the wall, it is a Peacenik. In fact, Conquerors have been known to pursue fleeing Peaceniks clear down the street in order to salvage what they perceive as a golden opportunity for a fight.

At the end of the day, regardless of motive, these people are out to have their own way. For those who have a penchant for dealing with conflicts in this manner, but feel they lack the necessary strategy, we offer the following Battle Plan:

Battle Plan for Having Your Own Way

1. Catch them off guard. Start an argument just as they are leaving for work.

2. Catch them at a disadvantage. Open discussions on crucial issues at a dinner party.

3. Set the stage by sulking. If that goes unnoticed, add a bit of sarcasm. Reserve hysteria for a last resort; it takes too much effort.

4. Monopolize the conversation. Hyperbolize issues. Avoid sticking to one topic, keep at least two going. Have a third ready if it looks as if you may have to yield the floor.

5. Use psychological or theological terminology as much as possible to label your partner's shortcomings (if they disagree, you can use that as proof that you are right). Get them to join with you in attempting to analyse how they got

that way. You might wish to end the argument by letting them know you don't wish to take advantage of their condition. You are only doing it for their own good.

6. Collect minor offences until you have enough for an authorized blow-up. Keep major ones for counter-attacks in the event of your partner wishing to confront you with a supposed offence. Once it is known that you have such an arsenal, communication can be kept very formal.

7. Keep it impersonal. Don't let the fact that you may actually love your spouse interfere with the fact that you are right. This could impede your perseverance.

8. Don't admit to being angry. Blow up later when they least expect it.

9. Keep issues black and white, right or wrong. Use a lot of absolutes, such as: always, never, and, every time.

10. It is poor form to remind your partner how frequently they have been wrong. Tell them how often you have been right. It's a much nicer put-down.

11. Use group situations whenever you feel the consensus of opinion may be in your favour.

12. Sarcasm is more effective if used in public.

13. Always be alert for new ways to undermine your partner's self-esteem. Devastating recollections can be triggered by single words. It is all in the interest of peace. If your partner doesn't have any self-confidence, you won't have any arguments.

14. Use questions as a trap, i.e., you might ask his opinion of nuclear war, then twist this around to prove he should cease arguing with you.

15. Quote others frequently to prove that what you are saying is not only your opinion. Phrases such as 'everyone thinks...' or 'all our friends...' or 'the entire church...' are heavy equipment.

16. Be absolutely sure to lay the blame for everything that goes wrong on your partner. Then judiciously mete out condemnation, rejection or avoidance to fit the crime—known as blaming and shaming for taming.

17. Don't back down from your point, in spite of the facts.

18. If the other person uses logic accuse them of being unspiritual. If all else fails, clam up and look refrigerated. If they still attempt to reason with you, stuff your fingers in your ears (in case you require your hands free, use last week's church bulletin).

People who are determined to be winners must remember that you can win the battle but lose the war.

Martyrs are people who give way. Often it is a protective device, but with people who do this as a regular pattern, one is tempted to assume that they have as much need to lose as Conquerors do to win. Yielding rights for the sake of a relationship is indeed a noble thing, provided we do not develop a Martyr complex and become resentful. It is frequently discovered that people who use this tactic have brains like computers, and when they finally do want to get their own way they can produce a very accurate print-out of all the conflicts they have yielded in for the last seventeen years.

Giving way is sometimes a very insidious tactic, because it is, in a manner of speaking, a way of implying that you are in control. You cannot give what you do not have. Conquerors frequently use this tactic when they see they are running out of ammunition, to avoid the bitter taste of defeat. Martyrs frequently hope to gain 'spiritual' capital by appearing to be behaving in the most 'Christian' manner. Yielding is frequently used simply as a tactic to shame one's partner into changing their mind in a conflict. Martyrs are frequently nothing more than covert Conquerors who have finely tuned the art to make it socially acceptable in Christian circles.

Horse-traders are the people who feel that the most noble thing in the world is compromise. Give a little to get a little. This sounds like a very mature approach to life. It seems logical that there should be give-and-take; consequently, a very reasonable approach would seem to be to work out our priorities and hopefully trade some of our low-priority desires in order to bring the higher-priority ones to fruition. It seems reasonable, possibly even spiritual. However, as an overall philosophy of a relationship, it is neither.

It is not spiritual, because the criterion is our own priorities, and we tend only to view the outcome as successful when we have bought cheap and sold dear; that is, when we have been able to give away a low-priority item to gain a high-priority item. This usually finds us peddling our low-priority items as though they had a high market value, like a schoolboy trying to trade his asparagus for someone else's chocolate cake.

It is also not very reasonable, because we find that all too often the values, desires and even quality of life that we are trading in are much more important to us than we had at first thought. And this is the real cost of a relationship. The more undesirable the issues that we have to endure in order to live with another person, the more costly the relationship. For instance, let us assume that all the issues are very black and white, totally desirable or totally undesirable: she wants to live in the city, and he wants to live in the country; a Pentecostal church versus an Anglican church; holidays in the mountains or holidays at the seaside; a Mini versus a Jaguar; Country and Western music versus Beethoven. If the only answer is compromise, then we have a week at the seashore and a week in the mountains; this Sunday at a Pentecostal church, next Sunday at an Anglican church; tonight we listen to country-and-western, tomorrow night, Beethoven. On these types of issues, compromise could

75

clearly cost you half your life. City versus country living, and a Mini versus a Jaguar, can obviously be compromised by some halfway measures, like, a house in the suburbs and a Ford Sierra. However, as long as the blackness and the whiteness of the issues remain, neither partner is satisfied. However, the cost of the relationship can be reduced.

Unifiers are committed to unity, not uniformity. They see their goal as blending interests, philosophies and ideologies in order to rule out the necessity for horse-trading. However, blending takes communication as well as motivation. Unifiers are deeply committed to the relationship, but they demonstrate their commitment without obliterating their own identity. They are willing to give way or withdraw, as necessary, and even to compromise on a temporary basis. Winning is not always enjoyable for them unless they see it as a victory for the relationship, not just personal one upmanship. They are willing to talk for hours in the hope of understanding the relative merits of country-and-western music or Beethoven. They are willing to assume that their partner has some valid insights that they may have overlooked when considering what size car to purchase, or whether to live in the city or the country. Worship services are important enough to them to draw up long lists of positive and negative qualities, likes and dislikes, on their choice of church. They recognize that individual expression is important, but that God has called them to a partner who will enhance that expression. They recognize that compromise no longer exists once we are able to appreciate and to some degree enjoy the tastes and views of our partner.

What do you get with such blending? Consider Dave and Carita. Do you get a goal-oriented procrastinator? No—in the case of Dave, you now have a young Lutheran pastor who recognizes that one of the best ways to meet effectively the needs that he is so sensitive to, is through efficiency, while with Carita you have a woman who recognizes that she now has the new tool of sensitivity to aid her in achieving her goals.

It may seem all well and good to talk about blending philosophies, temperaments and tastes, but what about all the little issues that come day-in and day-out, and tend to bring us to boiling point? How do you handle boiling point conflicts?

This takes confrontation. Confrontation skills enable us to talk to our partner without either internalizing our anger or blowing up—neither of which we can afford to do. We have a biblical mandate to confront one another. Matthew 18:15 says, 'If your brother sins against you, go and show him his fault, just between the two of you. If he listens to you, you have won your brother over.' The same thing is also true when the situation is reversed. Matthew 5:23 states, 'If you are offering your gift at the altar, and there remember that your brother has something against you, leave your gift there in front of the altar. First go and be reconciled to your brother; then come and offer your gift.' God desires relationships with no barriers, no hidden agendas, and no strings hanging off that our adversary the devil can pull and cause the relationship to unravel. Matthew says that if you have something against your brother—you go. If your brother has something against you—you go. Confrontations are necessary and biblical; they are our responsibility. Christianity gives us no mandate to sit back and hope that someone else will bring up the issue. Once we are aware of a problem, God has given us the responsibility to address it. In fact, we can conclude from the Matthew 5 passage that God considers mending relationships more important than religious activity.

First impressions are important, and it is always worth working out our wording in advance to ensure that we do not erect barriers that may make resolution of the conflict impossible. We may feel more vulnerable if we open up a confrontation by talking about ourselves rather than about the other person, but it is the safest route in the long run. If I begin with an 'I' message rather than a 'you' message, the other person is more at ease. A statement such as 'I have a problem I think you can help me with', does not carry the connotation of blame. This is more than just a gimmick, because if something is bothering me, I *have* a problem.

Mick and Dorothy came on a Christian Marriage Weekend out of curiosity. They felt they had pretty good communication. On their survey, they stated that they realized that they 'had not even scratched the surface'. There were some problems with their family roles, the way they saw their relationship to each other, and they both had low self-esteem, which was very inhibiting when it came to discussing sticky situations. However, they claimed an 80% improvement in their marriage just through learning how to begin an effective confrontation.

The words 'I have a problem...' appeared several times as couples have written back to say they are now free to enter into what they had previously considered 'dangerous waters'.

The second most important part of confrontation is the behaviour description, that is, separating the behaviour of an individual from the character of an individual. For example, it is not necessary to call a person a liar to communicate certain inaccuracies in their statements. It is the old axiom of 'separate the sin from the sinner'. Frequently, when parliamentary procedures are broadcast, it sounds like a veritable free-for-all, but there are limitations. For a start the individual's worth as a person must be upheld by addressing them as the 'Right Honourable Gentleman' or the 'Right Honourable Lady', and then you cannot say, 'The Right Honourable Gentleman is a liar', you must say, 'The Right Honourable Gentleman is misleading the House'. Learn to communicate in terms of problems and not character.

Another important thing to bear in mind is that you must not receive a confrontation and give one at the same time.

For instance, if a wife is disturbed by the speed at which her husband continues to drive, and she expresses it by saying, 'I feel very insecure out here in the fast lane the whole time. Do we have to go ninety miles an hour?' it is inappropriate for him to retort, 'Let's get the facts straight—who was responsible for the last three collision repairs on this car?' This is an evasive manoeuvre in the form of a counter-attack.

There are all sorts of problems with this tactic. First of all, it is saying, 'You are not qualified to talk to me about shortcomings. Get the beam out of your own eye first.' This may sound scriptural, but it is used out of context. Secondly, it converts a simple challenge to do better into a statement of condemnation, and at the bottom line it is a selfish admonition to, 'Get out of my life'. The wife, in this case, had had to make herself vulnerable in order to make the confrontation, and every time we violate someone's vulnerability, we erect one more barrier to communication.

Some basic commonsense procedures are, first, check out your own motivation—is this really for the good of the other person, or the good of the relationship? Are you willing to speak the truth in love? Second, select an appropriate time; see what kind of mood your partner is in and be sensitive to the fact that they may be dealing with other issues that are already draining a lot of their emotional energy. Third, define the problem, i.e., 'I feel insecure at ninety miles an hour.' Fourth, listen carefully to what the other person has to say; be attentive and sensitive. There might be an answer such as, 'Sorry, dear, I just want to get ahead of this long string of lorries before we go into a single lane.' Fifth, find areas of agreement and disagreement, such as, 'Yes, that seems reasonable, but we have been in the fast lane for an hour now.' Sixth, identify your own contribution to the problem, such as, 'You may think it's important to travel at high speed, but I fail to understand why speed is so important. It makes me so nervous.' Seventh, state positively what you might be able to do to help: 'I know I do a lot of back-seat driving, but this is the thing that bothers me

79

most. I'll try very hard not to comment on your driving if you'll just go a bit more slowly.'

Remember, God is not as interested in getting us through conflicts as he is in how we respond to them. He is more committed to our character than he is to our comfort. He is involved in the process of conforming us to the image of Christ, which means he is like a divine sculptor chipping off all the pieces of our lives that do not look like Jesus. Our mate is probably God's divine sandpaper to smooth off the rough edges.

Chapter 6

Differences

The very fact that men and women were created physically and psychologically different could lead any thinking person to suspect there might be a difference in social roles. However, we live at a time when the philosophy of the age and scientific fact are as far apart as they have ever been. What we perceive to be scientific fact (and our perception of theology) is greatly coloured by our own desires, wishes and morals. We frequently find that objective measurement has some degree of subjective flaw. This is especially true in the age of emerging woman's rights. The very mention of differences in ability between men and women, is very threatening to the feminist movement because it tends to imply superiority and inferiority, rather than just difference. Both male and female researchers in this field find that they are under constant pressure, and those publishing results which demonstrate differences find that they are bombarded by hostile phone calls and letters. One researcher who found evidence to buttress the theory of male aggression stated that 'this result was so striking that I sat on the data for a year before publishing'.

Testicles and ovaries, the legal distinction between women and men, are nothing compared to the fact that women carry the offspring. And that task brings with it a vastly different and highly complex set of endocrine and metabolic equipment—so complex, that not only are psychologists in the dark as to the full impact on women's behaviour, but physiologists are not really sure what is going on from a physical chemical standpoint.

We do know a lot about the effects of the menstrual cycle. And a most obvious and important fact is that women have their psychological ups and downs. Once a month their performance is impaired, depression sets in, anxiety arises and self-confidence lowers. We are tempted to feel that everything that goes wrong around the house can be attributed to pre-menstrual tension, post-menstrual tension or menstrual tension. In other words, it is an excuse for not co-operating. But that is not so, and if we were observant and discussed this openly, we would find a definite pattern and we would be able to act accordingly.

An awareness of this, for both husbands and wives, is extremely important. At different parts of the menstrual cycle, mood variations can more easily be recognized for what they are. For instance, Joyce finds it much easier to cope with a mood depression when she is about to speak at a large gathering of women, once she works out the fact that she is three or four days away from her period, and understands that she is suffering from a normal hormonal imbalance. Otherwise, she is tempted to feel that the Spirit dwelling in her has gone on holiday. It is incidences such as this that make James Dobson's book, *Man to Man about Women* (Kingsway Publications), highly profitable reading for both men and women.

It would be totally wrong to think of women as simply men with different plumbing and special equipment for carrying babies. Actually, every cell in our body has a chromosome combination which is masculine in men or feminine in women. Woman normally outlive men by three to four years. Their metabolism is lower than that of a male. Their skeleton structure does not only differ in their pelvis: they generally have a longer trunk, shorter head, broader face and less protruding chin. Men have smaller kidneys, liver and larger lungs. Men's blood has 20% more red blood cells, which gives them a greater supply of oxygen and consequently a greater constitutional vitality. Men are 50% above women in brute strength, their pulse is usually lower than women and their blood pressure is slightly higher.

There now exists a vast bank of data which indicates that male and female hormones precipitate more than external sexual characteristics. They actually masculinize or feminize the brain. Therefore mental functions vary between the sexes. Women have greater verbal ability. They speak earlier and more fluently. Boys stutter more, their spelling is worse, and they are more frequently classified as 'learning disabled' or 'hyper-active'. However, boys have a distinct advantage in visual, spatial orientation. They have a keen interest in manipulating objects and in geometric design. In early years, boys and girls are approximately equal at arithmetic, but when it comes to higher mathematics, boys generally pull ahead. Studies show that boys are more aggressive than girls, they invariably play rougher. Girls have superior tactile sensitivity, even in infancy, which may explain why in romantic situations, women are aroused by touch over their entire bodies, and male sensitivity tends to be limited to the genital area. Women tend to excel in fine motor coordination. This capability, however, does not limit them to needlework; it would be equally advantageous in something as exacting as brain surgery.

Researchers have determined that men tend to be more 'laterally' orientated in their brain functions. That is, in men, thinking processes are controlled either by the right or left hemisphere of the brain. Women's processes seem to diffuse through both hemispheres. This was first observed in studying brain damaged patients. Women showed less functional loss, regardless of which side of the brain was injured. Some believe that this is due to the fact that activities are duplicated in both hemispheres of a women's brain. Female patients suffering brain damage are much less apt to have speech impairments than men. And even female babies who are born with brain damage are able to cope with the defects better than males.

Thus, men's brains are said to function laterally, using the right or left hemisphere, while women tend to think 'globally'. The difference in male and female visual and spatial orientation, mathematical ability, and verbal predisposition is all attributed to this phenomenon. For instance, the fact that women think 'globally', may tend to slow them down in specific problem solving with higher mathematics, but it also explains why they are able to be much more intuitive than men. Intuitive thinking is simply the art of taking all the facts into consideration almost simultaneously. Researchers have also noted that female infants are more alert to social situations, respond more readily to facial expressions, and are better able to interpret the emotional context of speech before they can understand language. For this reason, we counsel as much as possible as a couple. Joyce is more sensitive to 'halo data' (moods, voice inflection, and body language).

It should be noted, however, that any specific difference that can be observed on an average between the sexes, is far smaller than differences within each sex. In other words, men may be on average 20% superior to women in higher maths, but the men at the top of the spectrum may be as much as 400% superior to men at the bottom of the spectrum. And the variation of mathematical ability among women will be equally as striking. Consequently, it is not surprising to identify one instance after another where a woman is far superior to a man in mathematics, or even a small group of women superior to a small group of men. But this does not negate the fact that, on a large national sampling, mathematics is an area of brain function where men excel. Nor does the fact that we may know a lot of men who have superior verbal skills negate the fact that this is an area of brain function where, overall, women excel. Individual instances and smaller samplings are cited by people who are 'grabbing at straws' in an attempt to disprove any differences between the sexes.

It is interesting to note that much of the research that has brought these facts to light has been conducted by people who would probably like to be able to prove that differences in behaviour between men and women are culturally induced. Scientists today are faced with a great controversy over 'nature or nurture'. Are men and women different because of learned behaviour, or are they different by nature (because God made them that way)? All of the data regarding the influence of hormones on behaviour tends to disprove the theory that masculinity or femininity is learned behaviour. Therefore it is a threat to the feminist argument.

The nearest feminists have come to providing scientific evidence for the supremacy of nature over nurture is a complicated theory known as a 'backloop' between thought and action. Studies on male Rhesus monkeys show that testosterone levels tended to drop when they suffered a social setback and rise when they had experienced triumph. Even with this, it is counter-productive to the feminist cause, because it would seem to emphasize that men have a greater ability to be men, the more they function in the way that they were created to function.

We have a large bank of scientific fact, the result of faithful research by people who are not the least bit interested in proving that God created men and women with different talents, abilities and dispositions to fulfil different roles; and yet we allow feminism to make such drastic inroads into our thinking that even many Christian wives feel guilty because they are not competing in the market place. It is the job of Christian husbands to help their wives appreciate the life-shaping importance of their careers as wives and mothers. To do this, they must first demonstrate that they appreciate that career for what it is.

It is our personal conviction that women would never have found it necessary to form a liberation movement if men had only assumed their responsibilities in the manner in which God intended, because a good deal of their complaints *at least* stem from men shirking their responsibility. The philosophy of the age has encouraged men into bizarre actions and gross overreactions, and it is impossible to determine any so-called 'norm' in our society. Today society offers no guidelines for family roles. Consequently, we are left with no alternative but to return to the Maker's Manual. But we must do this with no preconceived ideas from either this century or the last. The nineteenth-century notion of male superiority created the twentieth-century feminist backlash. Both are unscriptural. You will find nothing in the Bible which precludes men from washing dishes or women from carrying out motor repairs. We must follow the biblical principles for family roles and responsibilities, but we dare not attempt to turn our own preconceived ideas into theology.

For further consideration

Can we identify any differences of opinion which could be traced simply to a difference in masculine and feminine thought processes? How can we take advantage of this difference?

Chapter 7

Adam's Image

God created man in his image—which means he obviously
passed along certain attributes of himself into mankind.
But since man is less than God, we are still left with the
question of exactly what God intended mankind to be. And,
even more specifically, what is masculinity? Unfortunately,
we do not know a lot about Adam. We do know that he was
an able gardener and that he must have been very imaginative to be able to name all the animals. He was also rather
discriminating, because it seems he knew better than to
pair off a hippopotamus with a giraffe, or an orang-utan. It
is interesting to note that, although Adam had never seen a
woman, he was evidently born with some inbuilt 'programming' which gave him some notion of what she ought to
look like and enabled him to discriminate against all the
vertebrates which did not come up to this expectation—
which means we obviously do not need *Playboy* magazine to
tell us what we are looking for!

In the Living Bible Adam's proclamation of acceptance
reads, 'This is it!' Adam exclaimed. 'She is part of my own
bone and flesh. Her name is "woman" because she was
taken out of man' (Gen 2:23). If Adam had been an
American, he would probably have said, 'Wow! You *really*
know what you're doing, Father—I couldn't have done

87

better myself.' Of course, if he had been British, he would have straightened his tie and said, 'Now she's a bit of all right!' Adam had probably no difficulty in understanding his relationship to the animals in the Garden of Eden, but this was an entirely different situation. She was like him, but different (he obviously noticed the difference). Now the plot had thickened; as a homo sapiens amongst animals he had been comfortable with his different role. Now he was to find out what it meant to be a male amongst homo sapiens. He evidently did not have a thorough understanding. For instance, he did not realize all the implications of the concept of responsibility, for example, that 'the buck stops here', because when God confronted him on the issue of the tree of knowledge of good and evil, his immediate reaction was, 'It's this women you gave me.'

The Bible does not tell us a lot about the life of Adam and Eve. We do not understand much about their personalities. However, the Bible does tell us that Jesus Christ was the last Adam. We believe it does this for a very specific purpose. The recorded history of Adam as a perfect man (before the Fall) is very limited. God wants us to know in depth what it means to be a man as God intended men to be. God's concept of masculinity is Jesus Christ, the last Adam and therefore the last perfect man. (Clearly Christ's example was for the benefit of both sexes, but men have the advantage—perhaps because they need it more?— of having the model of a perfect man.)

Because this is a chapter on men's roles, I (Dave) am writing this in the first person. We feel it is much more realistic that men speak to men about being men, just as Joyce will be writing the next chapter in the first person from her own feminine perspective.

As evangelical Christians we are frequently so caught up with the defence of the deity of Christ, with the fact that Jesus was God in the flesh, that we tend to lose sight of the fact that he was man; not just man as in mankind, but also a male. As such, he was not only God's message to us of perfect humanity, but a message to men on masculinity. I believe that Jesus Christ was a man's man. He was not a 'sissy', nor would he have been the little skinny 'wimpish' looking character so often portrayed in medieval paintings. If the Bible calls him the last Adam, it means he was a perfect man—spirit, soul and body. He was not a sissy, but neither did he have to drink twenty pints of beer in an evening to prove his masculinity. Jesus Christ was God's concept of masculinity, in the flesh.

Although we are aware that we live in a humanistic society, we frequently forget that that society is so far removed from God's ideal that we can have no concept of the extent to which issues are clouded, and our reasoning is blurred because of this rebellious mind set. One of the issues which seems to be a greater problem to men than to women is the idea of occupational stereotypes. Women seem to be able to go out to work and, for the most part, be simply women who are out at work. Men, on the other hand, seem to be much more vulnerable to occupational stereotypes. We know what the popular image of a shop steward is, and of an executive. We have our idea of a solicitor, a regimental sergeant major, or a fighter pilot, and we tend to model ourselves after these stereotypes. Some of these are perfectly valid. A bank manager, for instance, is a very precise, but also very cautious, individual who methodically questions each step of a proposition. He seems to have a 'nose' for ferreting out potential problems, and at times I get the idea he is making a mountain out of a molehill. His personality is at the opposite end of the scale from some of my fighter pilot friends. They have a totally different personality, which their occupation encourages. They do not fly safe distances over the tops of mountains, but they roar down through the valleys and twist and turn around the mountains, because they were taught to fly low level, under the radar, and, if necessary, just ignore the flak. I do not think my bank manager would do too well under those circumstances. Even if he had the training, his mind set would be too far out of step. On the other hand, if my bank manager tended to throw caution to the wind, like my fighter pilot friends, I would probably change banks.

Occupational stereotypes exist because we observe that there are certain types of people who get ahead in certain occupations. However, this has only limited validity, because we must not lose sight of the fact that behind each one of these occupational stereotypes is a real man.

Take, for instance, a regimental sergeant major who understands his men, understands the mission, knows the necessity of discipline and training and whose years of experience have given him insight into how to motivate men. True, in a mass situation some of this motivation is achieved by a lot of bellowing in order to break up inertia and get men into motion *now*. Unfortunately, the young soldier who has his heart set on becoming a regimental sergeant major and who models himself after this man, will frequently lack the discernment to copy the finer points of his personality, and will probably begin with the most obvious characteristic, which is bellowing. And all we have then is a loud-mouth who lacks understanding; and, of course, the only thing worse than someone who does not know what he is talking about, is someone who does not know what he is talking about at a hundred decibels.

Maturity seems to take ages as we painstakingly collect data, copying characteristics from first one model and then another. There is no such thing as instant maturity, but Christians can certainly shorten the process by going back to the Manufacturer's Manual.

Headship is uniquely masculine. This, from a family perspective, is not a role that we can observe in the life of Jesus. However, the concept of headship is something that he was certainly involved with. Headship means simply to establish course and maintain it. This, of course, is what management and leadership are all about. We might be tempted to say that we can observe in the life of Christ that he was equally at home as a supervisor or as a servant, but that would be inaccurate, because Jesus saw being a supervisor as being a servant.

God's concept of management is servanthood. Jesus said, 'The greatest among you will be your servant' (Matt 23:11). Jesus did not suffer from the 'Big Boss' syndrome. He did not operate in the mode of leadership-through-tyranny, nor even the speak-softly-and-carry-a-big-stick type of leadership. Jesus was a servant and he underlined this in John 13, through the object lesson of washing the disciples' feet. At one point Jesus directly contrasted servanthood with the world's view of authority. He said, 'You know that those who are regarded as rulers of the Gentiles lord it over them, and their high officials exercise authority over them. Not so with you. Instead, whoever wants to become great among you must be your servant, and whoever wants to be first must be slave of all' (Mk 10:42b–44).

From these scriptures, we can establish a principle that authority was never given for the benefit of the person in authority, but only as a tool for serving those under authority. The concept of serving those under authority even holds true in a secular situation where the goal is to manufacture a product. The employees have committed themselves to this purpose and are most fulfilled when the purpose is accomplished. The supervisor who can motivate each individual to fulfil his potential (through discipline, if necessary) is, in fact, serving the group by ensuring that all assets are related to the goal and that nobody's talents are abused.

Once it is understood that a leader is a servant in the true sense of the word, the people under his authority recognize that he is interested in their well-being. They know that they can trust him to ensure that they are properly rewarded and that their grievances are given a fair hearing. They know he will make sure that work is fairly distributed and see to it that those with superior performance are rewarded and when possible promoted, and those with inferior performance are fairly dealt with as well. Once they understand this, they no longer have to spend their energy ensuring that they are fairly treated, and they can direct their energy towards the goal their leader is desiring to attain. This is biblical leadership in its pure sense. Sometimes we get glimpses of this from men who have some concept of it, but all too often we are influenced by wrong models.

This concept of leadership is to be carried out in the home in the form of headship. The Bible tells us, 'Husbands, love your wives, as Christ loved the church and gave Himself up for her' (Eph 5:25; Amplified). This love includes keeping and providing for. Paul continues: 'However, let each man of you (without exception) love his wife as [being in a sense] his very own self' (Eph 5:33, Amplified).

There are very good reasons why God gives this command to love our wives. It addresses a basic weakness in men. Love means meeting needs; it means giving my wife, and ultimately, the family, what they need and not necessarily what I want to give them. Men tend to set some very selfish, self-centred goals. They are the head of a corporation, the family, and frequently their notion of what that corporation is supposed to produce or accomplish fails to take into consideration the needs of the rest of the family members. These goals, although they may in reality be Dad's ego-trip, may seem to be defensible in terms of the whole family. But having the biggest house in town and making the most money, although it has carry-over value for the family, does not in itself meet the family's needs. And there are other goals that are harder to defend, such as: the goal of this corporation is to produce the world's best golfer (Dad). Is that not reasonable? Should my wife not be thrilled to be Mrs World's Best Golfer? Would that not meet her needs?

In the United States, in almost every area of the country, we have a fish called the large-mouthed black bass, and with the exception of a few trout purists and salt-water fanatics, this is *the* sport fishing trophy. There are some exceptions but, generally speaking, bass grow bigger the further south one travels.

When I was in my early thirties, lean promotion prospects kept my job from being very fulfilling. But I saw the way to personal gratification through being a bass fishing expert. I was good at it, approaching the problem very methodically and scientifically, and gathering copious amounts of data, hoping to persuade the University of Florida to allow me to do a master's degree in 'what makes a fish bite'. I had actually developed a form for the purpose of recording this data on every bass weighing over four pounds that I caught. It had a space for water temperature, surface conditions, air temperature, barometric pressure, and even the position of the sun and the moon, which have a bearing on relative animal feeding-times. I made all of my most successful baits, some of my fishing rods, my tackle box, and customized my boat. I did none of these things just for the fun of doing it. Each item was purpose-oriented. I was learning to think like a large-mouthed black bass. Joyce said I even smelt like one! It was gratifying to pull up to the boat dock with my tackle, which, although customized, was very unpretentious, and heft out a string of large fish, when the guys with the big, classy rigs had only a few minnows for their trouble. My picture was in the paper and on television, people even popped into my office during the day to ask advice, and everyone wanted to fish with me in the hope of gleaning some secret knowledge. One of my high points was the day the Colonel in charge of qualifying all the bomber pilots on the base went fishing with me. He did not fish for the most part, he just paddled the boat and watched me fish.

My family was involved in this to some degree. Joyce was a pretty good fisherman, and the children could hold their own. We had some wonderful outings on various Florida lakes and rivers; but it has probably become obvious to you by this time that real bass fishing was far too serious a business for a family outing. I can remember one time when our youngest son actually had the nerve to fall overboard when I was casting towards what I thought was a particularly large specimen. Consequently, most of my fishing expeditions were done without the family. The children were proud of their dad's notoriety, and I did manage to make fishermen out of both my boys; but I now realize that there were a lot of other values I would have done better to have passed along to them. I did not give Joyce and me a lot of time together, either. Being out on a lake at night with nothing but the sound of bullfrogs and crickets can be romantic, but Joyce did not always see it that way as she silently paddled the boat while I exercised my night vision casting under cypress trees (the big bass struck better at night). Somehow I feel that producing the best bass fisherman in town was not a goal that met my family's needs.

This command for husbands to love wives addresses a basic need in women. This bass fishing business illustrates that men derive their sense of self-worth from being respected for their competence. This is important to women as well, but not nearly as important as a sense of belonging. Lord Byron said, 'Man's love to man's life is a thing apart; 'tis woman's whole existence.' This makes women much more sensitive to the state of the relationship, and low self-esteem and depression are frequently the results of women being neglected by their husbands.

This command is also a way of fleshing out the gospel, because it illustrates Christ's relationship with the Church. Many people have difficulty with the concept of God as Father because they have never known a real father. Also, many have difficulty with the concept of the Church as being the Bride of Christ, because they have never actually seen anything but battered brides. Husbands who actually do love their wives as Christ loved the Church provide a working model of the gospel.

It is only by loving their wives that husbands can properly fulfil their authority role. God's idea of authority as servanthood means that winning the admiration of those under authority is a prerequisite to their submission.

Women are required to submit, but most men seem to be more familiar with the verse that says, 'Wives, submit to your husbands', than they are with the commands that are directed toward them. Most of us never dream of winning our wives' submission, but just simply demand it—'It's in the book, woman; submit!'

One of the most important tools of leadership is communication. The leader is responsible for effective use of all the assets under his control. The skills, talents, judgements and insights of a wife are part of those assets. Any man who consistently makes decisions without consulting his wife is missing a valuable perspective. 'So God created man in his own image, in the image of God he created him; male and female he created them' (Gen 1:27).

God created man in his own image—which means he passed along certain selected qualities of himself to his new creation. However, since men and women are different, evidently he did not pass along all his qualities to one sex. God speaks of himself as masculine; he is the Father. We have no problem with that. But he also speaks of himself as having a mother's love (Is 66:13). Some of the qualities and insights of God are uniquely packaged in our wives, and any husband who fails to take advantage of this is guilty of poor stewardship.

Eve was created to be Adam's helpmeet. Consequently, if a husband is to take full advantage of his wife's gifts he must share problems with her; not just family problems, but problems in their own lives, personal issues that they are dealing with. If you are dealing with a personal issue in your life, you can be sure that your wife is aware of it to some degree. What she may not be aware of is exactly the amount of concern that it is causing you, or she may not know whether you are actually dealing with it or just hoping it will go away. Lack of communication only creates anxiety and gives her an opportunity to believe the worst.

1 Peter 2:13–3:7 deals with authority from many angles. It culminates in a passage which says, 'Husbands, in the

same way be considerate as you live with your wives, and treat them with respect as the weaker partner and as heirs with you of the gracious gift of life, so that nothing will hinder your prayers' (1 Pet 3:7).

Because of the context, we can determine that when Peter speaks of the wives as being 'weaker partners', he is not talking about spiritual, psychological or physical strength, but is speaking of a position-orientation to authority. Authority is a position of strength; submission is a position of weakness. It is very difficult to submit all your talents, energies, and other assets to someone who has no apparent respect for them. Many men have learned this first-hand on their job. I did a tour of duty in Vietnam. As a hospital administrator advising the Vietnamese how to run a hospital, I was teamed up with a physician who was almost an exact carbon copy of Major Frank Burns in the 'M.A.S.H.' television series. I have frequently considered writing a secular book about the way this man carried on. He was quite unqualified for the job he was doing, and was totally inept at it. He was also thoroughly gauche and rude, and was not respected by his fellow physicians or anyone who came into contact with him. But worst of all for me, he was my immediate superior. All my time, talents, insights and energies were at his disposal. I was away from my wife and family for a year, and I wanted to make this time count for something. But all my eggs were in his basket, and unfortunately for me, he was playing 'catch' with the basket. It was an extremely frustrating period of my life. I was given a medal at the end of my tour, but not for bravery. The Colonel who put me in for it stated that anyone who could put up with this particular physician at close quarters for a year without punching his lights out, deserved a medal.

A couple of years ago, we received a frantic phone call from a woman who needed to be seen right away. She would not come to our house, and we could not go to hers. She met us in the village half-way between, and began to pour out her fears and frustrations regarding her marriage and her family life. The reason for such a clandestine meeting was that she absolutely did not want her husband to know that she had discussed these matters with us. When I asked her why she had discussed them, she said it was either that or commit suicide, she was so frustrated. Eventually we were able to persuade her to allow us to talk to her pastor to see if he could persuade her husband to submit to marriage counselling. The pastor was overjoyed; he had been aware of this problem for some time, but had always been forbidden to speak to the husband. However, he was not very excited about calling the man in, because, from all that he had heard, this man had real problems and could be an absolute tyrant.

However, he made arrangements for the man to come to the manse one Wednesday evening at seven-thirty. I showed up at seven o'clock, and we began to pray and discuss; we even arranged the seating in the room so that one of us could block the door if he tried to bolt before we had finished putting our proposition to him. We were well aware that once we began to bring up his marriage, we would probably have to scrape him off the ceiling. He arrived at the appointed hour, and was a little surprised to see me. The pastor said, 'Dave has something to share with you.'

I gulped, and told him that evidently his wife had lost all confidence in their ability to communicate over crucial issues, and that she had come to us as an alternative to committing suicide.

He very calmly asked, 'What do you suggest?'

I told him that he needed counselling, he needed someone to just sit down with them and go through some of these issues, to act something like a traffic cop to help them through crowded intersections. I also added that it did not really matter who did this. Joyce and I were not looking for business. The pastor immediately interjected that he was not looking for business, either. The man decided that we would be the best ones to do the job, since we knew him the least well and could probably be more objective.

On their first session, we asked them to do a simple homework assignment, which at first sounds very negative. We asked them each to make a list of fifty failure factors: he should write out fifty ways he had failed as a husband, and she should write out fifty ways she had failed as a wife. We hoped that once they saw these issues, they would know where to begin. They returned the next week. He had thirty-seven factors written out. She only had sixteen, and the sixteenth one was, 'I guess I don't know my own shortcomings.' That homework assignment, however, broke the back of the problem. When this woman looked at her husband's list and realized that he recognized and was concerned about every one of the issues that she was concerned about, almost all of her anxiety was washed away. She had been all too willing to believe the worst about him, which is a sin. However, he had deserved it; he had given her no cause to believe anything else.

I see a principle in 1 Peter 3:7. The way to respect a weaker partner is to let her know how much you respect all that she has placed under your authority; the way to really love a woman is to give great attention to letting her know with what a humble sense of stewardship we are handling her contributions towards the marriage, and encouraging the development of her gifts. Joyce has put all her eggs in my basket. She deserves to know how I am handling the basket. I feel this is a great demonstration of love, because it is a mechanism for removing anxiety from a relationship. 1 John 4:18 tells us, 'Perfect love drives out fear.'

For further consideration

Someone has said, 'Authority is like a bar of soap. The more you use it—the less you have.' What does that statement mean to you?

Chapter 8

Priorities That Produce the Product

We have likened the marriage union and the resulting family to a corporation, and every corporation produces something. We find a very specific statement in Malachi regarding God's expectations of this particular corporation. 'Has not the Lord made them one? In flesh and spirit they are his. And why one? Because he was seeking godly offspring. So guard yourself in your spirit, and do not break faith with the wife of your youth' (Mal 2:15).

God desires godly offspring. If we have children, our involvement in the Great Commission of Matthew 28:19 starts at home. However, even a childless couple can produce godly offspring. We are all told to 'go and make disciples'. This does not mean that a childless couple must adopt children, in the normal-family sense. But in a spiritual sense, there is a vast army of 'abandoned children': people who have been evangelized, but deprived of a 'Christian upbringing'.

We are well aware that many couples do not feel qualified to disciple others. However, taking God's desire for godly offspring seriously does not necessarily mean running out to find a 'Timothy' to disciple. Some must start at a lower level. They must concentrate on establishing themselves in the faith and equipping themselves for ministry. Another way of acting upon the Great Commission is to become involved with ministries which are committed to making disciples. Godly offspring is the product of the corporation, and we must not lose sight of this goal. A family does not exist solely for the benefit of the family, any more than a hospital exists solely to give medical treatment to its staff members.

Having said this, we must realize that to reach this goal, we need to have priorities. God has set priorities which not only ensure that the product will be produced, but that the corporation will be protected, as well. It is very logical that if the producing unit is not protected, it will not be able to produce.

Priorities are just that—priorities, and not ironclad rules. They indicate the normal mode of operation. Priorities can be circumvented in an emergency and for special purposes, but only on a temporary basis. When we find we are regularly circumventing our priorities, we must admit that we are not circumventing them, but violating them. For instance we intend to spend time alone with God each day. If we fail to do this approximately once a week because of extenuating circumstances, we can certainly claim to live according to our priorities, since this is our normal mode of operation. However, when this 'quiet time' is something that only happens about 50% of the time, we have to question our commitment to our priorities.

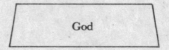

The chart for priorities is to be viewed as a series of building blocks which represent the priorities that God has laid down in his word to accomplish his purpose through family life.

100

The basic building block is our relationship with God. The first of the Ten Commandments states, 'You shall have no other gods before me' (Ex 20:3). When Jesus was asked what was the greatest commandment, he replied, '"Love the Lord your God with all your heart and with all your soul and with all your mind." This is the first and greatest commandment' (Matt 22:37–38). Obedience to this commandment begins with actually working on the relationship, speaking to God, expecting him to speak to us, in our hearts and through his word. And it continues on through the day as we live according to his principles and priorities.

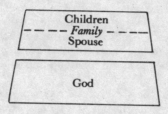

The second block is the family block. It could well be divided into an upper and a lower tier, because the priority relationship, the basic relationship within the family, is our spouse. We have a command, 'Husbands, love your wives, just as Christ loved the church and gave himself up for her...' (Eph 5:25). Can there be any doubt in a husband's mind that his wife is his priority relationship in all the earth, second only to God himself? Women have the command, 'Wives, submit to your husbands as to the Lord' (Eph 5:22). And also, 'Now as the church submits to Christ, so also wives should submit to their husbands in everything' (Eph 5:24). This should leave no room for doubt in a wife's mind that her relationship with her husband is second only to her relationship with God.

The relationship between husband and wife is the highest relationship amongst human beings spoken of in the Bible.

It is the only relationship where God ever said the two shall become one. Occasionally we give the children, who belong in the top tier of the family block, priority over our partner. But this is a violation of God's priorities, and it does a great disservice to the children as well, because it breaks down their resident model of a marriage relationship. When a relationship with children takes precedence over a relationship with our partner, family life is reduced to the level of the animal world. Preservation of the species amongst human beings is produced by the preservation of family life. This begins with the integrity of the relationship between husband and wife. It ensures that when the children grow up and have their own offspring, they can bring them to visit Grandma and Grandpa, who are still living together in the same house. Family relationships which put children first tend to break up when the project of raising children is completed, because the husband and wife have nothing in common.

Nevertheless, the children take priority over everything else. 1 Timothy 5:8 tells us, 'If anyone does not provide for his relatives, and especially for his immediate family, he has denied the faith and is worse than an unbeliever.' 1 Timothy 3:4 states, 'He must manage his own family well and see that his children obey him with proper respect.' How can

anyone command respect of children and inspire obedience unless they pass along their life values to them? And how can they pass along their life values unless they invest time in them?

The next block could be labelled our 'public'. God has a definite interest in how we meet our public—the people we interact with every day. This block could also be split into an upper and a lower tier, the lower tier being our occupation. We gain a testimony through how we perform at our job. This is not limited to husbands who go out to work. The occupation of being a housewife and mother sometimes comes under more scrutiny from the world than the husband's occupation. Paul talks about occupations in several passages. In Colossians 3:22–41 he says,

> Slaves, obey your masters in everything; and do it, not only when their eye is on you and to win their favour, but with sincerity of heart and reverence for the Lord. Whatever you do, work at it with all your heart, as working for the Lord, not for men, since you know that you will receive an inheritance from the Lord as a reward. It is the Lord Christ you are serving. Anyone who does wrong will be repaid for his wrong, and there is no favouritism. Masters, provide for your slaves what is right and fair, because you know that you also have a Master in heaven.

As employees, we are to have a respectful, effective and productive relationship with our employers. And as employers, we are to have an effective, respectful and caring relationship with our employees. This passage tells us that the relationships will be judged, whether labour to management or management to labour. There is also a second and very logical reason for this priority, and that is that we spend eight hours a day with our peers witnessing to them in everything we do. How can we possibly have a good testimony if we are 'skiving off' and they are doing half our work as a result?

This passage has the potential for debunking another

great misconception, if only we will listen. We can serve the Lord in a secular occupation. One does not have to be employed in so-called 'full-time Christian work' in order to be spiritual. We have a tendency to look on our occupations as necessary evils. Men frequently consider that they are selling 40 hours of their life each week for the financial means to sustain them during the other 128 hours. Very few have the sort of vision that sees that a secular occupation can be a form of ministry. Being a housewife or a carpenter to the glory of God is as important in God's economy as preaching.

The upper tier of this block is our neighbours, which includes the people we come into contact with each day, like the people in the shops, the milkman, the postman, etc. How well do we relate to them? What kind of a testimony do we have before them? 'He must also have a good reputation with outsiders, so that he will not fall into disgrace and into the devil's trap' (1 Tim 3:7).

The speed with which we settle our accounts with local tradesmen, the way we maintain our lawns and gardens, and the thoughtfulness that we show to our neighbours, are all measuring devices of the effectiveness of Christ in our life.

104

Many are puzzled when we announce that the top block, with the least priority, is our ministry, especially since this is the obvious place where the product is produced. There are two logical reasons for this. The first we have already mentioned—it is that if the corporation fails, it will no longer produce a product. The second is the fact that if we have children, the product—disciples—may well be being produced in the family block. Peter addresses this in 1 Peter 3:15–16. He makes it very plain that we are to be equipped for ministry: 'Always be prepared to give an answer to everyone who asks you....' But he also adds, 'Keeping a clear conscience so that those who speak maliciously against your good behaviour in Christ may be ashamed of their slander.' This means that a ministry stands or falls upon the credibility of our lives in respect to these other priorities. It also means that the words that we have to share are so powerful and, in many instances, so disturbing to people in the outside world that they will be grasping at straws, looking for any excuse to reject our message. Consequently, they will be attempting to malign even our good behaviour. We must not let any poor behaviour on our part provide them with a legitimate excuse to speak maliciously against us. If our marriage is falling apart, our children strung out on drugs, our house in such a poor state that it is actually running down the value of property in our neighbourhood; if we fail to pay our bills on time and are not respected in our occupations, we cannot have a ministry. That is why God gives us these priorities—they enable us to have a lifestyle that will support a ministry.

One area where confusion continually arises is our relationship with God and our ministry. We frequently confuse our ministry with our relationship with God. This is particularly so among clergymen and those with leadership responsibilities. It is very easy to do, and it almost sounds logical: 'If God has called me to preach, then preaching is my number one priority.' However, the person who makes that statement must remember that God called him to be a husband, a father, an employee, a neighbour, and *then* a preacher. And obviously, before any of these, God called him to be his child; he called him into a relationship with himself. This must be maintained, first of all, followed by the other relationships in descending order of priority.

David and Rosemary Meikle heard us speak at Royal Week and contacted us some time later to talk through some marriage problems they were having. David is the rector of a large Anglican church in Ipswich, and this is a very demanding job. When they unfolded their story to us, it became clear that, to some degree, David was married to his job. He could not refuse anyone at any time. Part of his problem was that he had not known that he should. He had not realized that Rosemary had a right to expect that a certain amount of his time should be spent with her and the family. He knew that she had a need for this, and it tore at his heart that he was not meeting it. However, he felt that God would to some extent make up the deficit. But this was a deficit that was continually mounting and drawing interest. They were both very relieved and excited to know that in God's eyes their marriage relationship took precedence over work. After going through the priority blocks in this chapter, we gave David a homework assignment. He was to preach a sermon on God's priorities in family relationships. There were three reasons for this piece of homework. First, if someone has to teach a concept to others, he has to get a good grasp of it himself. Secondly, we felt that after this sermon, if he explained to someone that he needed time for his family, they would understand what he was talking about. Thirdly, we were able to listen to the tape and thereby be assured that he had got the message. This turned out to be one of the most important messages he preached in that church.

There is another insidious thing about ministry: often it is not just that we feel God has called us to a particular task, but that we have, to some degree, actually made a god out of the ministry. The ministry has become an extension of ourselves. It has become a way of bolstering our faltering ego, and unfortunately, some of the time the things that we call 'ministry' are really just 'ego-trips'. And there are even times when 'ministry' is used as an excuse to avoid family responsibility.

God did not save us to serve: he saved us to have a relationship with him (our number one priority). He did not send his Son into the world to recruit workers: he already had a vast army of angels. Ministry is a privilege that God extends to us because he knows it gives meaning and purpose to our lives.

Some feel that all the blocks do not apply to them. Pastors, for instance, frequently feel that their occupation and their ministry are one. However, this is not always a realistic concept. Most people who are employed in Christian service are employees. As employees, certain jobs are expected of them which are not necessarily to do with ministry. The office of vicar in the Church of England is notorious for this. Social and administrative expectations greatly limit effective ministry. When we find ourselves in this situation, we have a responsibility respectfully to challenge our employer's priorities; but we still have a responsibility to carry out the mundane tasks of this occupation with a right heart attitude.

One rector and his wife in Norfolk once shared with us that there was not one Christian in either one of the churches for which he was responsible. Not only were there no Christians, but, they said, 'These people are so hard-hearted and cold that no one else will go near the church.' They were naturally very distressed about this, mainly because they had perceived that if there were a more friendly congregation some of the other villagers might come and hear the gospel. They were positive that there were people who were searching. We discussed their priorities and asked them to view them from a layman's perspective. His occupation was to lead two very dead churches that 'did not want to know'. He had an occupational responsibility to fulfil the office of parish priest and a responsibility to God to preach the gospel. His dilemma was that the place where he was employed was not an effective platform to reach people who were vulnerable to the gospel. We explained that if he were a layman, he would work forty hours a week at a job which in and of itself would not necessarily make contributions toward the Great Commission, and that when he came home at night he would be looking for a way to reach out to his neighbours. Since the church at that time was not an effective outreach, we suggested that they use their home.

They 'imported' a few live Christians from another village and invited half a dozen unchurched villagers for a 'social evening', which included a few choruses, some sharing, and a lot of fellowship. The villagers thought the evening was a marvellous idea and elected to do it again in a fortnight's time. This was the beginning of a sharing group which eventually totalled seventeen villagers. It also formed a ministry opportunity which allowed a husband and wife to minister together.

Ministering together is not always possible, but it is an objective to be seriously considered for the obvious reasons that it provides one more area of common interest and allows more time to be spent together. Also, discussing goals and directions for the ministry automatically involves examining values, which itself precipitates meaningful communication—and this is invigorating to a marriage relationship.

Gordon and Doris Westbrook, who are both school head teachers, and are both involved in the church, came on our very first weekend because they felt that their individual involvements were robbing them of time together and were also taking them on somewhat divergent paths. Consequently, when we asked them if they would consider working with us on the Weekends, they saw this as a golden opportunity to minister together and to think and work and plan together. Although they only do approximately three

Weekends a year, their involvement with the Weekends has given them a ministry to couples in their church, which means that they now counsel together. They have also dropped their individual ministries in the church in favour of leading a housegroup together. This concept of ministering together seems to be rather more important with couples who are both working outside the home.

Keith and Caroline Tondeur were experiencing some difficulties in their marriage. Keith works in London, in the stockbroker business. He is a natural achiever, with a great propensity to be a workaholic, and he works amongst workaholics; his colleagues hate to see the weekend come because then the Market is closed. Many of them are at their desks until seven o'clock at night, and may possibly spend another two hours in 'occupational socializing' at a local bar before catching their trains home. Add to this the fact that Keith has an hour's ride on the train, and you can see that little time was left for family involvement. When Keith came to Christ, he became convicted about his time away from home and he greatly reduced his 'overtime'. However, almost simultaneously he developed a false spirituality which caused him to believe that the things of this world were not very important, and he became rather complacent and uninterested in his occupation—which quite naturally caused repercussions down at the office.

Viewing this as an 'either/or' situation, he began to wonder if it would not be better to become a missionary, or do something more 'spiritual'. It seemed that if he put in the hours that pleased his employer, his family suffered; and if he devoted himself to his family, his career suffered. Then Keith came into a better understanding of God's priorities. He realized that the way he performed his job was a ministry. He prayed and asked God to give him wisdom and insight; and then he 'put feet to his prayers' and began to work very hard from nine till five—but drew the line on nearly all 'extra-curricular' activities. At first he had a lot of flak for refusing to attend some of the all-night parties and social activities designed to enhance business relationships. But God was faithful and increased Keith's productivity to the point where it was obvious that he did not need to work overtime, nor did he need the added leverage of cocktail parties. The last two times I saw Keith, he had been singled out for recognition for his productivity. He no longer feels that he needs to go on the mission field; he recognizes that he *is* on the mission field. He is the only gospel that many stockbrokers will be exposed to; and he takes this very seriously.

For further consideration

There are 168 hours in the week. It is an interesting exercise to begin with 168 hours and then subtract the time spent sleeping, time on the job, time in travel to and from work, time spent in the bathroom, time spent eating, at devotions, watching television, shopping, in church, reading, studying, preparing talks or sermons, gardening, hobbies, etc. List every activity done each week or likely to be done. See how much time is left over for time alone with your partner and each family member, as well as for family group activities.

Chapter 9

What About Eve?

What is my role as wife?

Where am I getting my input for that role?

Do we realize how much the world influences our thoughts about husband and wife relationships? To what extent is our subconscious mind programmed by television and women's magazines? Psalm 1:1 says, 'Blessed is the man that walketh not in the counsel of the ungodly' (AV). Perhaps the blessedness of family life has been lost because too often we have walked in the counsel of the ungodly.

When the term 'marriage roles' is mentioned, the automatic word association for most women is submission. This word has been reduced in the secular world to a grotesque caricature. Does being submissive actually mean being a 'door mat'? We need to look at the Manufacturer's Instruction Manual to see what the correct definition actually is and what our role as a wife is and how we are to function in that role.

Genesis 2:18 in the Amplified Bible reads, 'Now the Lord God said, It is not good that the man should be alone; I will make him a helper meet (suitable, adapted, completing) for him.' I am to be my husband's helpmate, that which is in me completing him, as we blend strengths and weaknesses to make one flesh. Then, after the Fall, God said to Eve,

'Yet your desire and craving shall be for your husband, and he shall rule over you' (Genesis 3:16). God established headship for the family with the first couple. The world does not believe or accept that, and would tell us that submission means inferiority.

A lot of Christian women feel anger rising in them when they hear about submission. I believe the problem comes from accepting the world's definition and viewpoint of submission rather than God's. Before we look at the wife's relationship to her husband, I'd like to look at Christ's relationship to the Father and see how it is similar.

Jesus said, 'I and the Father are one' (John 10:30). This speaks of their equality. He also said, 'For I have come down from heaven not to do my will but to do the will of him who sent me' (John 6:38). Though they were equal, Christ lived in submission. Paul cites this principle again: '[Christ] being in very nature God, did not consider equality with God something to be grasped, but made himself nothing, taking the very nature of a servant' (Philippians 2:6–7)— equal yet submissive. In John 5:30 Jesus states, 'By myself I can do nothing; I judge only as I hear, and my judgment is just, for I seek not to please myself but him who sent me'—not independent in the wrong sense, but pleasing the Father. The writer of Hebrews tells us, 'But in these last days he has spoken to us by his Son, whom he appointed heir of all things, and through whom he made the universe. The Son is the radiance of God's glory and the exact representation of his being' (Hebrews 1:2–3). Again, equal in status yet showing the headship of the Father. Jesus speaks of the unity that exits between himself and the Father: I have given them the glory that you gave me, that they may be one as we are one' (John 17:22).

So what is Christ's relationship to the Father? Equal to the Father, yet submissive, wanting to please the Father, united. Christ knew he was equal in status to the Father and being submissive did not make him inferior.

We need to look at the marriage relationship in the same

way. The Bible makes no distinction in the status of men and women: 'There is neither Jew nor Greek, slave nor free, male nor female, for you are all one in Christ Jesus' (Galatians 3:28). In Genesis 1:27 we read, 'So God created man in his own image, in the image of God he created him; male and female he created them.' Created equal in dignity and worth.

Though we are equals, in God's overall plan for orderly ruling, everyone has to submit to someone. Peter tells Christians: 'Submit yourselves for the Lord's sake to every authority instituted among men' (1 Peter 2:13). Slaves were to submit to masters or, you might say, employees to employers (verse 18). Colossians 3 talks about submission within the family: wife to husband, children to parents; and Ephesians 5:21 of Christian submitting to Christian.

We see this order of headship and submission laid out in 1 Corinthians 11:3: 'Now I want you to realise that the head of every man is Christ, and the head of the woman is man, and the head of Christ is God.' If there is going to be orderliness, someone has to be held accountable, there has to be a position of authority. We can take this one logical step further by adding the scriptural admonition for children to obey their parents. When you go into a home where the children are in control, it is anarchy. You are uncomfortable in such a place and glad to leave it. Likewise, it is uncomfortable to go into a home where the wife wears the trousers. You do not feel right because it is not God's order. Conversely, neither are you comfortable if you are under a man in authority, be it in the church or in the home, who himself is not under the authority of Christ. Submission does not mean inequality, as the world would have you to believe. It is God's plan for peace and order.

Though God has made us equal in dignity and worth, we differ in function and responsibility. What is my responsibility? How do I function in that role? Ephesians 5 gives us some basic guidelines. Ephesians 5:22 says, 'Wives submit to your husbands as to the Lord', and verse 33, 'The wife must respect her husband.'

What does it mean to submit? Be a doormat? Never have an opinion? Yes, dear. No, dear. Whatever you say, dear.

I looked up 'submit' in Roget's Thesaurus and I must say, it gave a whole column of words that connoted negative feelings. But that is not the scriptural view of submission. To submit is to yield, to give forth. If my role is to be my husband's helper and completer, I need to yield all that I am. Submission means giving your total self—your thoughts, feelings, input. It means communicating, sharing ideas, insights, fears, needs, dreams, using all the gifts God has given. If my role as wife is that of helper and completer, I cannot function if I do not communicate.

In many homes the husband and wife have a different focus: she, short range and immediate; he, long range. Her input is needed in the computer in order to get the complete picture, but she must remember that God has given her husband the responsibility, whether he wants it or not, of making the final decision based on all the data.

There is communication—and communication. I am not talking about nagging or criticizing. 1 Peter 3 says that a wife should have a gentle and quiet spirit. This is an approach and attitude that attracts. In other words, we need to learn how to speak to our husbands *without stirring up their old nature*. When this happens, I am afraid that it is because *we have been speaking out of our old nature* and have just been answered in kind.

We must not forget the other charge the Lord lays before us: that of respecting our husbands. Sometimes there is submission without respect, but the two go together. I can be submissive and do the right thing and completely blow it by how I do it. I also need an attitude of respect. I need to respect the position of headship that God has placed my husband in. I know that some wives find it difficult to respect their husbands because of their lifestyle, but you can still respect the position of headship and act accordingly.

Why does God ask me to respect my husband? It is

because it meets his need for significance and demonstrates an attitude of submission. My need is to feel loved, his is for significance, and how I treat him can help fulfil that need. This is circular thinking; if he would meet my need for love, I could meet his need for significance. At the same time, it is possible that he is saying, 'If she would respect me, I would find it easier to love her.' We cannot wait until our partner becomes obedient to the word. God holds us each responsible for living according to the light he has given us. I am told to respect my husband, so I need to get on with it and not wait until I feel loved by him. God will give me what I need to fulfil his commands. 'Faithful is he that calleth you, who also will do it' (1 Thessalonians 5:24, AV). God is always the power of his own demands.

Some may be thinking, 'How can I show him respect when I do not feel respect?' Our emotions are generally a by-product of our thoughts and that is where we have to fight the battle. When my emotions are less than spiritual, I admit it to the Lord: he knows anyway. He does not ask me to change my emotions, but my thought patterns. Chances are, my thoughts about my husband have become negative and critical. I am also holding some resentment about something he said or did or failed to do. In other words, I have not reacted in the right way to something that has happened. God does hold me responsible for my reactions, even if I feel I have been wronged.

I need to confess wrong thoughts and resentment, and ask the Lord to give me understanding. Each situation is different, but I may need to understand why David acted the way he did. Or I may need to understand myself better, to see why what he did irritated me. It may be the sort of thing that, when prayed over, can be discussed calmly. Many times we find that what happened was a complete misunderstanding and not something done deliberately to hurt.

Sometimes a lack of respect can be nipped in the bud as simply as this. It is when we do not watch our thought life that little incidents begin to pile up and what started as one little stone becomes a huge wall.

I know some may be saying, 'I wish the problem with my husband was that simple.' I have heard a lot of complaints: 'He is really self-centred; he makes promises he does not keep; does not assume any family responsibility; drinks too much; cannot manage his money; has a terrible temper. When you live with this year in, year out, and all you get are broken promises, you lose respect.'

True, that is how human nature responds—we are apt to lose respect in these types of situations. But when God said wives are to respect their husbands, he was not talking to our human, or old, nature, but to the new nature born of the Spirit of God.

God gives us a lot of supernatural commands: 'Love one another as I have loved you'; 'Accept one another as Christ accepted you'; 'Forgive one another as Christ forgave you'. Remember, he never asks us to do something that he will not empower us to do. His nature in us can enable us to love, accept, forgive—and respect. Have you ever noticed that it is the unlovely one who needs the most loving, the one who is acting obnoxiously who most needs to be accepted? Likewise, treating with respect someone whose actions do not deserve it, meets an inner need in them and often brings about change.

What I am trying to say is that if the Lord has asked us to act, to talk, to conduct ourselves in a respectful manner to our husbands, then through the power of the indwelling Holy Spirit, he will enable us to do so, if we are willing. This basic word is given to Christian wives and is not qualified by phrases such as, 'If he is a Christian', 'If he is worthy', 'If he treats you right'.

I mentioned earlier that respect is shown by our attitude —not just by what we say, but by how we say it. Let us look at some other ways we communicate respect.

I appreciate that David is a leader and can assimilate facts and make a decision quickly. My temperament makes me cautious and decision making is slow and painful. When I finally make a decision and start a course of action, I am besieged by all sorts of doubts and I wonder if I am doing the right thing. This has presented a problem in our marriage.

A man feels respected when he is supported in his decisions. David would come to a decision which I would agree with—at first. Then over the next few days I would begin to voice all the doubts that were surfacing. Consequently, David did not feel I respected his leadership and ability. I did really, but I did not understand just how different we were as far as the decision-making processes were concerned. I finally learned to keep my mouth shut and voice my doubts only to the Lord who with much patience would quieten my fears. Now I can be more vocal in supporting his decisions and leadership.

While I am on the subject, I will share another problem I had along these lines. David was always thoughtful about asking my opinion about things. I would share what I thought and felt about situations, but would assure him that I was just putting more information into the computer, that I appreciated the fact that he had the responsibility to make the final decision. Sometimes we would be at this stage and get interrupted. We would not get the chance to talk about it again until the next day when I would bring it up. Then he would accuse me of nagging but I really just had not had the chance to finish everything I needed to say. So now, when we are interrupted I say, 'I haven't finished yet.' Then we know we have to get back to it. Once I can talk through the thing, then I can let it go and trust the Lord to give David wisdom to make the right decision.

Submission can be a frightening thing to a woman's heart—especially if she does not believe her husband is looking to the Lord for guidance. This is why it is so important for us to be rightly related to the Lord—submitted to him, sharing every part of our lives with him, trusting him to give our husbands the wisdom described in James

3:17: 'But the wisdom that comes from heaven is first of all pure; then peace-loving, considerate, submissive, full of mercy and good fruit, impartial and sincere.' Pray that verse for your husband, trust God, and then support your husband in his decisions. A husband feels respected when he is trusted and knows that you feel he is competent for what ever lies ahead. Our husbands need our encouragement and backing.

One area where we fail to show respect to our husbands is in the way we conduct the household when he is away. I am referring mainly to the discipline of the children. As soon as Dad leaves, one of the kids will ask, 'Can I...?', knowing full well that Dad has already laid down a policy against this. But how many times do we hear ourselves saying, 'Oh, I guess so. It won't matter.' We do not realize it, but we have undermined our children's respect for their Dad because we ourselves have shown disrespect by not carrying out his wishes.

Making time for your husband makes him feel that he is important to you—another part of respect. It is so easy to get our priorities out of line and have time for the children, the house, committees, shopping, friends, hobbies—everything and everyone but 'hubby'. That can certainly make him feel left out. We need to remember that our husband is our number one priority on earth, and treat him accordingly.

Respect and loyalty go hand in hand. It is unfortunate that when women get together and start talking about their homes and families, their comments about their husbands are so often negative. 'My husband never...'; 'I wish my husband would...'; 'My husband is so...'. Sometimes I think the reason so many women are discontented in their marriage is because they sit around talking down their partner to a friend. I am sure the enemy smiles with glee when he hears two women cutting down their husbands.

Some years ago, when David was in the Air Force, he went on a remote tour to Goosebay, Labrador, for fifteen months. When he came back, it seemed as though he had gone in one direction and I in another, and we were strangers. I had a 'friend' who pointed out some of David's negative qualities to me. They had not loomed so large until someone else called my attention to them. I remember one day naming off all of David's faults to the Lord. I wanted the Lord to do something about them. Just then, the Lord broke into my monologue, not audibly, but speaking into my heart, and he said, 'Why don't you just give David to me, and let's work on *you*?' I was quite stunned, but I said, 'Okay.' I gave David to the Lord, and promised not to look at his life, but to allow the Lord to work in changing *me*. As I kept my focus on the Lord, I changed; and one day he let me look at David to see the change he had brought into his life, as well.

You know, I find the Lord still operates under the same principle after all these years. As soon as I start to complain to the Lord about something in Dave's life, I hear a 'Yes, I have noticed a similar root problem in you—just manifesting itself in a different way.' It is the old splinter/beam principle (Lk 6:37–42).

I know that sometimes you just have to talk to someone about your husband—you have to get it off your chest. Tell your friend—your best Friend. Because Jesus loves both you and your husband, he will give you some good advice and you will not be disloyal—you will not lose respect.

The Lord has made us to be our husband's helpmate, his completer, and a wife complements her husband as she brings into the marriage her unique differences to make one flesh. So often, though, we have the wrong focus. We live in a competitive society. As youngsters, we competed with our siblings. We competed in the classroom, on the sports field, and on the job. We come into marriage, and feel that we are competing with one another.

Why do we look at each other as though one has to be right and the other wrong? Why not see each other as being different—one complementing the other? We see things from different viewpoints, and we should capitalize on that difference, rather than let it become a wedge between us. A wife may see things with her heart and a husband with his head, and both are needed to get the complete picture. If I had sight in only one eye, I would lose perspective. I am grateful that the Lord blessed me with two eyes.

Imagine Dave and me seeing a large tree for the first time and describing it to one another. Dave is standing about two feet from the tree, looking straight ahead and describing the bark, the girth, the density. I am standing a bit further back, looking straight up into the branches swaying in the breeze, the green leaves fluttering with the sun filtering through.

Dave says, 'What do you mean, "swaying in the breeze"? This tree is stationary—it couldn't possibly bend in the wind, and it's too thick for any sunlight to come through.'

'Well,' I reply, still looking up, 'maybe your glasses are dirty, because *I* can see sunlight through the leaves.'

'Oh, you just *think* you see something moving.'

At screaming pitch: 'Are you calling me a liar?'

Does that kind of dialogue sound familiar? We are both right, of course; it's just that we each have a different perspective. Both views are needed to get the complete picture.

I guess when David and I got married, we must have brought in a spirit of competition without realizing it. When we had a difference of opinion, we seemed to feel that one had to be right and the other wrong. I would eventually get frustrated because I could not make myself understood, and would do the womanly thing—cry. (Most women cry when frustrated—men walk out.)

Finally, one day I could stand it no longer, and cried out to the Lord about our communication problem and what could I do. (This was long before there were any marriage books on the market and I seemed to learn everything the hard way.) The Lord helped me to see that if Dave and I had been brought up in the same small village and lived next door to one another we would still be different. Our parents, our families, our environment, teachers, the books we read—so many factors go together to make us each unique individuals. I needed to share with David that I was different and only wanted him to know me better. When I gave a different opinion, it was just that—different from his—and I was not implying that he was wrong and I was right. I was only sharing myself so he would know the woman he had married, and I was not trying to compete with him. When I shared this outlook with David, it changed both of us. I was no longer frustrated and he did not feel I was trying to get the better of him. If we are going to make the most of our differences, we need to understand and accept them. We found out it is more important to think together than it is to think alike.

I must admit that when first challenged with Ephesians 5:22: 'Wives submit to your husbands as to the Lord', I found it rather foreign to my nature. But over the years, I have discovered one of God's surprises. Submission, as God presents it in his word, brings joy and a sense of fulfilment —a confirming sign that this is God's order.

May I share with you a prayer someone gave me years ago that I still voice? 'Lord, help me to become the woman my husband needs in order for him to become the man you intended him to be.'

For further consideration

When Dave turned fifty, I made him a special birthday card listing fifty reasons why I was glad he was my husband. Fifty positive character qualities. It only took a short time, but I realize that some wives would have to bring all their powers of concentration to bear to compile such a list. However, I would suggest that the harder you perceive this project to be, the more urgent it is that you do it. If you already have a positive focus on your husband, you will have little problem. If your focus is negative, this exercise will help you to begin to think more positively.

Chapter 10

Money Speaks

Whether we have money left over at the end of the month, or month left over at the end of our money, is not as far beyond our control as some of us would like to believe. A lack of funds is almost never a reason for financial bondage. The real problem is a poor focus on material goods, which leads to poor stewardship.

The Bible speaks to many areas of our financial steward-ship and there are many books written which deal with this subject at depth. However, there are some major considera-tions which can be covered effectively in one short chapter and since a misunderstanding of the biblical perspective on material possessions frequently creates pressure in a mar-riage, we will discuss the concepts now. This chapter will show you whether you need to take more time to follow up the points raised.

We believe that the Bible teaches that God wants to bless us in this life. There are many promises of this. In the context of gifts and offerings, Paul says to the Philippians, 'And my God will meet all your needs according to his glorious riches in Christ Jesus' (Phil 4:19). However, there is no single-stranded cause-and-effect relationship, as the proponents of the 'prosperity gospel' seem to portray. 'Seed faith' is sometimes presented as planting a 'fiver' through

Spirit-directed giving and harvesting a hundred pounds later. We are sure this has happened many times as an act of God. However, when prosperity is presented in this single-strand fashion, it has been stripped of some major considerations. In fact, it may shock many to realize that this simplistic reasoning has actually reduced financial reasoning to a level of humanistic logic. Humanism operates in only one dimension—the horizontal: we invest in order to receive. The Christian perspective requires that we invest with no thought of receiving. However, we can do this because we are aware of promises such as 'God will meet all your needs'. Having our needs met and planting a money tree are two different things.

If we wish to approach finances from a biblical perspective, we must begin by understanding the more general, all-encompassing precepts, and only then can we hope to apply correctly the single-stranded concepts. Matthew 6:33 has been made into a popular chorus by Karen Lafferty, so most of us have memorized it effortlessly: 'Seek ye first the kingdom of God, and his righteousness; and all these things shall be added unto you' (Matt 6:33, AV).

The kingdom of God is where God is King. Jesus said, 'The kingdom of God is within you.' Seeking the kingdom of God, then, quite naturally involves being obedient to God in every area of our life, which means that the concept cannot be a single-stranded issue. Consequently, a biblical perspective on finances does not begin at the thin end of the wedge and work its way up. It starts at the thick end of the wedge and works down. It begins with, 'What are you doing with your life?' and works its way down to good stewardship in the grocery store; and at no point does it look for 'returns', only for needs to be met. We would like to lay out a few of these concepts for your consideration, beginning at the thick end of the wedge.

1. First of all, make it your desire and objective to bring every facet of life under the Lordship of Christ. This will involve living a life which fleshes out the claims of Christ,

which is the most effective tool in lifestyle evangelism. It also means being committed to the Great Commission to help others to maturity in Christ.

2. Transfer ownership of all your assets to God. This involves not only money and possessions, but earning power and our time itself.

There are several reasons for this. The most obvious is that we really cannot call Christ 'Lord' and at the same time consider our assets, car, home, bank account, etc, ours to do with as we please. It is a bit patronizing to tell God we will allow him to use our car for a certain project—especially since we should really be grateful to God for letting us use his car to go back and forth to work in, or for our holiday.

A second important reason is that God takes good care of his property. And we in turn will take much better care of God's property if we look on ourselves as stewards rather than owners. Back in the sixties, when a lot of antiques sold for a little more than used furniture and grandfather clocks, copper kettles and warming pans were between one-tenth and one-twentieth of their present value, we furnished our home with these items. We picked up bits of English and Dutch Delph, Chinese porcelain, and other breakables, to give colour to the decor. You might have guessed what happened. These things have gone up in value to the point that we cannot even afford to insure them properly. But all the time this was going on, we had an 'open home' ministry. We have had as many as a hundred young people in the house at once (a bit of a squash) and, let's face it, young people do not always use their heads; they wrestle and tickle one another, they throw pillows, trip over things, fall into things, and spill drinks on things. However, through all of this, God has protected *his* property. The old furniture and china give the place an elegant warmth that makes everyone feel at home, and they are an effective tool in our ministry. God has done a good job at protecting these tools against what some might consider insurmountable odds!

3. Establish the Bible as the final authority in financial

policies, as opposed to the philosophy of this age. What society regards as acceptable and normal is no more a basis for action in finances than in morals.

4. Establish the practice of tithing as a reminder that everything belongs to God. Many see tithing as purely an Old Testament concept, and this is not illogical when one considers that everything does belong to God. However, it is obvious that God dealt with the nation of Israel in a far more regulatory manner than he deals with the Church. Individual Jews did not have the indwelling Holy Spirit as each individual church member does. Consequently, they were a nation who lived by ruled and regulations. If God felt that 10% was a minimum that could be imposed across the board with the people of this nation, who he treated in an almost juvenile manner compared to the Church, how can we accept less? We can only start with 10%, fulfil our obligations, and then seek God about how to handle any surplus.

Malachi 3:10–11 tells us to bring our tithes into the store house. However, in this age, when the Church has so many specialized ministries and missionary societies, there is some ambiguity about exactly what the storehouse consists of. Is it strictly the local church? Christian ministries? Widows and orphans, or poor people in distress? The Bible certainly has more to say about providing for the needy than about giving to the structures of the Church.

It is not good stewardship simply just to drop our tithe indiscriminately in the lap of any church or organization which claims to be a Christian ministry. We must consider the following: do their goals take the Great Commission seriously? Are they relating their assets to their goal? It is one thing to have a goal and another to relate to it. Just as we as a family establish a goal, for example, 'to be an example of godly living' and, through our financial policies, relate our assets to that goal, so must an organization that is worthy of our support. Sad to say, there are many organizations which have their roots in evangelical Christianity, but which have lost sight of their goal. Someone has said that once an organization passes the twenty-year mark in its existence, it is in grave danger of becoming merely a monument to its founder, presumably because the second generation does not have the same vision. Fortunately, there are hundreds of exceptions to this rule. We are told that there are missionary societies in this country which have tremendous funds but have great difficulty in recruiting missionaries, while others, short on funds, have long waiting lists. It is obvious that young people willing to give their lives to go on the mission field want to go out under a society whose policies, actions and emphasis support their goals. Which brings us to the next point: are they gaining positive results? Are people responding to their message? If people are responding to the message and their goal takes into consideration the Great Commission, then not only are disciples being produced, but the organization will be reproducing itself as well.

5. Evaluate expenditure in terms of achieving your goals. For instance, I think if we were setting up house in the 1980s, we would probably use reproduction furniture rather than antiques. We now live in an age when one can buy a respectable and reliable wristwatch from £20 to £10,000. There is no doubt in my mind that I need a wristwatch to function effectively in my ministry. But there is a point of diminishing returns on value for money. This brings in a cardinal principle:

Separate *needs* from *wants*.

6. Develop sales resistance. Our modern age, with its mass media, seems to have only one goal in mind: to raise the lust factor in every human heart. We find ourselves believing we need things that we did not even know existed, and sometimes buying things that we really cannot use, as well as things that do not do what they claim to do. Frequently we buy things we could just as well rent: a caravan, for example. Some people use their caravan enough to justify its purchase, but other people just have their caravan

depreciating in their back garden.

Frequently we are so blinded by this lust factor that we fail to find out if the product can be purchased more reasonably. I (Dave) spend a considerable time sitting at my desk. Therefore, I felt it would be a good investment to buy an office chair that fitted me well and would hold up under prolonged use. I found a little factory that made leather furniture and ordered a chair for £130. It was a lot of money—but I am convinced it was a good investment. Over the last ten years, I have probably sat in it a total of three years. A few months after I bought it, I happened to be down in London at a very exclusive department store and spotted the same chair, made by the same factory, for a little over three times the price. There is obviously a broad range of prices for the same item, but not usually that extreme. Sometimes, of course, other things have to be taken into consideration, as well as price. For example, one item may be slightly more money at one shop than another, but the first shop may offer a better follow-up service.

Another way of keeping the lust factor in check is to commit the need to God and give him an opportunity to demonstrate his power and love by providing it. A good rule of thumb is to identify the specific item needed, ask God to provide it (through ordinary or extraordinary means), and then begin a special fund to purchase the item. At least twice during our marriage we have seen people buy washing machines on hire purchase, only to be offered one free a few days later by someone who was moving. This brings us to the next item.

7. Make it one of your financial goals to get out of debt altogether and never borrow money for depreciating items. 'Let no debt remain outstanding, except the continuing debt to love one another' (Rom 13:8a). Proverbs 22:7 tells us, 'The borrower is servant to the lender.' James 4:13–14 tells us that we are not to presume upon the future. Hire purchase presumes that we will have at least the same income level next year as today; which might make it

difficult to respond to God's leading. It is one thing to have a house mortgage, which is money borrowed on an appreciating item, and another to hire-purchase a houseful of furniture, which are definitely depreciating items.

8. Give yourself breathing space. Do not spend every last penny. We like to think of our finances as divided into three areas: budget, back-up and bank. 'Budget' is our current account, where we keep the necessary funds to pay our monthly expenses. 'Back-up' is a small deposit account of £200–£400 which is an emergency fund. There is enough to handle a small unforeseen disaster, like replacement of a boiler, a major car repair, a major appliance replacement (but not all at once!). If we have saved this up in advance the sudden disaster will not throw us to the loan sharks. The last account—'bank'—is the real savings, our investment. It may be a building society or another special deposit account. This is where we save for another car, or a holiday, or a down-payment on a house. It is also the place where we have funds that we can afford to give away.

This last account is an area of our finances, and an area of our life, that needs special consideration in terms of stewardship. It is one thing to save for a particular item; it is another to save just to get rich. We, quite frankly, do not have that problem. But there are some who do. There are some who have a house that is paid for and every material item they want, with tens or even hundreds of thousands lying in stocks or in the bank. We have the distinct feeling that large sums of money held in this way will *not* be an asset when we account for our lives.

God has a purpose for our finances. They are a very special tool, both in dealing in our lives and through our lives. Through our finances, he can give direction to our lives, he can unite us with other Christians as we meet needs or have our needs met, he can build up our faith as we see him operate. Through our finances he can reveal his power and faithfulness, and this frequently serves as a witness to others who are looking for tangible evidence that God is alive. It is also through his financial blessing to us that he intends to finance his earthly ministry.

Financial freedom is freedom from the pressure of debt, freedom from preoccupation with material possessions, and freedom to obey God.

Financial freedom is not always financial independence. John and Sheila came on a Marriage Weekend and recognized that they had problems in communication; but this was because there were a lot of tensions in their lives that were drawing them apart instead of uniting them. One of them was the fact that each had a job and they had separate bank accounts. On the Weekend they recognized that the priority of one-ness in a marriage relationship did not mean losing individual identity, but it did mean sacrificing individual rights. One of the steps they took was to sacrifice the financial independence of 'his-and-hers' bank accounts for 'our' bank account. A small thing, you might say, but one more commitment to the relationship.

Jim and Rita had separate jobs, but they scarcely had enough money to justify *one* bank account. They came on a Marriage Weekend because another couple paid their way and loaned them a car to come up in, as well as minding their children. They stated that they also came with a lot of arguments, a rebellious attitude, and a lack of ability to express themselves. They realized that their lives were not really committed to Christ at any point. Each lecture seemed to be directed specifically at them. They did commit their lives to Christ, but because finance seemed to be their biggest problem, they made a special and tangible commitment in that area. Part of it was to get out of debt altogether. When they arrived home, they found a cheque from the Inland Revenue for a little over £500. This represented an overpayment on one particular year's taxes. Shortly after that, another cheque of approximately the same size came through their letterbox. This enabled them to pay off their debts and to start from a firm scriptural foundation. This tangible demonstration of God's sovereign power strengthened their resolve in all other areas. They are one of our best advertisements for Marriage Weekends.

Financial bondage means having to delay paying bills and being enslaved to businesses or investments; it is having more faith in material possessions than in God, and consequently choosing material·gain over inner character. It involves taking life models from materially successful people rather than godly people and striving for 'successful' friends as against godly friends. In the end it involves adjusting our ethics to suit our finances.

Brian and Susan Evans work with us on the Marriage Weekends. Brian is a successful insurance broker. He started in the business as an unbeliever with an unbelieving partner. They worked their way up to doing £1½ million of business in a year. But there came a time, after Brian's conversion, when he began to see the wisdom of Paul's admonition not to be unequally yoked with an unbeliever. It seemed that in both personal and ethical areas he was being challenged every step of the way. When he first shared with his partner his idea of dissolving the partnership, his partner violently disagreed with him. He told him that if he left, he would have to leave empty-handed. Brian thought and prayed about this for a long time. Was his faith resting in God, or in his material possessions? Could he and his family stand a radical change in lifestyle? Could they start all over again from scratch? As time went on, his conviction became more sure. He would have to trust his prosperity completely and totally to God. In the end, his partner was a bit more conciliatory, but still Brian started out with little to build on. However, two years later his present business now operates out of three offices in three towns, employing another fifteen people. Brian is a natural business man, and he has a wife who backs him every step of the way. Like Keith Tondeur, he is the only gospel that many will read; but the gospel is there, loud and clear, and in bold type.

Money speaks, and God uses any language he can to communicate the gospel.

For further consideration

Are we in financial bondage? How can we avoid hire purchase? Are we being good stewards of our income, or are we saving up for a rainy day on a par with the Great Flood?

Chapter 11

Emotional Trading Stamps

I (Joyce) am writing this chapter in the first person because it is a very personal issue, and there is great danger that in using writing styles which allow expressions to come from two or more people, something may be lost. It becomes much easier to intellectualize, doctrinalize, and therefore depersonalize, an issue. Aside from that, by temperament I am just a little more vulnerable in this area than David is. I can handle anger or simple irritation in three ways: I can blow up, clam up or use this emotional force to initiate action that will resolve the problem. Thankfully, as we have grown in the Lord, we both use the last alternative more frequently. However, I am much more prone to internalize anger, while it does not take much astute observation to recognize even mild irritation in Dave!

People who clam up, or internalize their anger, are for the most part just collecting emotional trading stamps. When the page is filled with the little brown stamps, we feel that we have enough for an authorized blow-up—so look out! Sometimes we are keenly aware that there is someone against whom we are saving stamps. We may have a page for our husband, a page for mother-in-law; and then a page for a neighbour and a page for someone down at the church, etc.

Ephesians 4:26 tells us, '"In your anger do not sin": Do not let the sun go down while you are still angry,' and then it goes into the next verse saying, 'and do not give the devil a foothold.' The passage gives some very specific instructions about dealing with anger. It is especially directed towards those of us who have a tendency to clam up. We cannot allow problems to hold over until the next day. We have to deal with them then and there. I think the word is very specific here, where it says, 'Do not let the sun go down while you are still angry,' and gives a reason—so the devil will not gain a foothold. If we do not clear it up that day, the next day, after sleeping or brooding on it, it is even worse.

Late one Saturday night about ten years ago, when friends who had been visiting us had gone home, Dave and I were sitting at the kitchen table having a drink before we went up to bed. I began to share a new insight that I had had into a particularly emotionally-charged dilemma; but because of something that I had not realized, Dave thought the remark was manipulative and felt it was 'hitting below the belt'. Whereupon he really lost his 'kingdom living'. To vent his frustration, he smashed his glass on the table. I thought, 'Well, two can do that!' and I threw mine down, too. Oh, that felt good! I had never tried anything like that before. Dave got up and stormed out of the house, and I put my feet up on the table and sat there, stewing. I just could not get over how I was feeling—I was really angry.

He finally came in, and said, 'Go on up to the bedroom.' I said, 'Fine. You clean up the mess, and I'll be glad to go upstairs.' I got into bed and began to catalogue all the reasons why I was angry with him, and all the things that had happened, and the list got longer and longer. It went from the immediate problem to all sorts of things against his character. And then I realized what was happening. And I said, 'All right, devil, I don't need any help from you—I can make up my own list!' I was still very angry, and I told the Lord, 'Lord, I'm not mad at you. There's nothing between you and me—it's just *him*.' Of course, I knew that was not right. In fact, I had taught on this subject before, a number of times. If you are out of sorts with somebody on the horizontal, you are automatically out of fellowship with God vertically. Then this verse came to my mind—'Do not let the sun go down on your wrath.' But, of course, the sun had already gone down, so I had a whole day! And since I did not feel that I normally got my share of blow-ups, I was going to make the most of this one. Legalistically speaking, I had a whole night and a day before I had to get things right and apologize.

In the meantime, Dave was down in the kitchen cleaning up the mess, not at all sure he wanted to come up to bed. He was thinking, 'Boy, if she snivels or starts making some peace overture, I'm going to go sleep in the guest room!' He was not ready to make up; but little did he know I was not about to snivel! I was not ready to make up, and I was not anywhere near tears. We were both very angry, and we went to sleep that way.

The next day was Sunday. We had to go to church. Fortunately, neither one of us had any responsibility at church. We had both cooled off, but we could not talk about it yet. After we came back from church, we were finally able to ask each other's forgiveness and to realize that it was all a misunderstanding, as is so often the case. Dave was able to tell me why the remark was so upsetting, and I was able to assure him that there was no hidden 'agenda' in my remark, I had just been sharing an idea.

Anger is a terrible force, and unless we deal with it scripturally, it is very apt to colour our entire mental process. The enemy is right there to make all the mileage he can out of situations that are not properly dealt with. When we allow offences to go unresolved and unforgiven, we build walls.

Unforgiveness builds walls and it creates bondage. It builds a wall between myself and the person who has hurt me; but even worse, it puts me in bondage. I am in bondage to the offender, I am in bondage to the situation, I am in bondage to my own bitterness. If I am bitter towards an individual over a certain offence, all sorts of little things keep bringing him into my mind. Every mention of the person, his occupation, the area where he lives, every piece of data that would plug into the offence, all bring the situation flooding back. I am in bondage to this person. Whether I am trying to eat or sleep or concentrate on another matter, I cannot escape. And all because I am not willing to forgive. It builds and builds, and begins to fester in my mind, in my heart, and in my spirit. It puts up a wall not only between me and the offender, but between me and God.

Forgiveness is non-optional. God does not give us a choice. Nor does he have any special category of offences or offenders that do not need to be forgiven.

Conversely, when we allow forgiveness to come into our heart, it builds bridges and it gives release. Jesus gives release to us as we forgive the individual involved, because he in turn is able to forgive us.

Unforgiveness is competing with God's authority. It is assuming a right that can only be exercised by God, and one which brings a terrible penalty when assumed by men. 'But if you do not forgive men their sins, your Father will not forgive your sins' (Matthew 6:15). This is a very definite and frightening statement. God has two sides on which he can be approached: his justice side, or his mercy side. This statement tells us that unforgiveness on our part disqualifies us from approaching God on his mercy side. We can only approach him on the basis of justice. I for one do not want justice from God; I want mercy. This theme is reiterated over and over in the New Testament. Just ahead of the verse I've just quoted, in the Lord's Prayer, we find, 'Forgive us our debts, as we also have forgiven our debtors' (Matthew 6:12). Forgiveness is not only non-optional, it is proportional. Every time we pray this prayer, we are asking God to forgive us in proportion to our forgiveness of others.

Matthew 18 is a chapter which Christians love to quote,

especially verse 19, which tells us, 'If two of you on earth agree about anything you ask for, it will be done for you by my Father in heaven.' However, this word 'agree' in the Scripture is something much stronger than simply two people having the same desire. It is the word from which we get our English word 'symphony', and we know that with a symphony we must have harmony and precision, co-operation and timing. Therefore, it is not remarkable that this verse is sandwiched between two passages dealing with relationships: the brother who sins against you (verses 15–18), and the parable of the unmerciful servant (verses 21–35).

Then Peter came to Jesus and asked, 'Lord, how many times shall I forgive my brother when he sins against me? Up to seven times?'

Jesus answered, 'I tell you, not seven times, but seventy-seven times.

'Therefore, the kingdom of heaven is like a king who wanted to settle accounts with his servants. As he began the settlement, a man who owed him ten thousand talents was brought to him. Since he was not able to pay, the master ordered that he and his wife and his children and all that he had be sold to repay the debt.

'The servant fell on his knees before him. "Be patient with me," he begged, "and I will pay back everything." The servant's master took pity on him, cancelled the debt and let him go.

'But when that servant went out, he found one of his fellow-servants who owed him a hundred denarii. He grabbed him and began to choke him. "Pay back what you owe me!" he demanded.

'His fellow-servant fell to his knees and begged him, "Be patient with me, and I will pay you back."

'But he refused. Instead, he went off and had the man thrown into prison until he could pay the debt. When the other servants saw what had happened, they were greatly distressed and went and told their master everything that had happened.

'Then the master called the servant in. "You wicked servant," he said, "I cancelled all that debt of yours because you begged me to. Shouldn't you have had mercy on your fellow-servant just as I had on you?" In anger his master turned him over to the jailers to be tortured, until he should pay back all he owed.

'This is how my heavenly Father will treat each of you unless you forgive your brother from your heart.'

This passage is lengthy, but very dramatic, because Jesus deliberately uses a very absurd contrast; absurd in terms of real life: one man being forgiven several million pounds and failing to forgive just a few pounds. Jesus uses this seemingly ridiculous contrast because although it may seem outlandish in human terms it is a true spiritual parallel. Compared with the number and magnitude of sins that God has forgiven us, what we are asked to forgive is nothing at all—it accurately compares with the contrast in this parable.

Frequently we act as though we can nurse a grudge, hold on to bitterness and anger, and still walk with God, still be blessed. And yet this passage clearly tells me that I have to forgive my fellow man if I am to know the forgiveness of God.

Forgiveness recognizes the sovereignty of God. From the cross, Jesus said, 'Father, forgive them, for they do not know what they are doing' (Luke 23:34a). Jesus knew that the Father had a plan for his life which was part of his plan for the world, and that these men, in executing him, were in reality executing God's plan. God has a plan for our life, as well. That plan is for us to be conformed into the image of Jesus. This does not happen in a vacuum. Character is never developed in comfort. When we are offended, we must remember the sovereignty of God, and that the offender is merely a tool in God's hand, chiselling away un-Christ-like qualities in our life.

Forgiveness also recognizes the sovereignty of God as we understand that God deals with the offender on our behalf. As Paul says, 'Do not take revenge, my friends, but leave room for God's wrath, for it is written: "It is mine to avenge; I will repay," says the Lord' (Romans 12:19).

When we forgive, we are recognizing that if the person needs to know how insensitive, unthoughtful or rude they have been, God will make this known to them. This is why the passage goes on to say, 'On the contrary: "If your enemy is hungry, feed him; if he is thirsty, give him something to drink. In doing this, you will heap burning coals on his head." Do not be overcome by evil, but overcome evil with good' (Romans 12:20–21). In other words, godly behaviour on our part will do much more to underline an individual's guilt than our direct action.

Forgiveness is separating the offender from the offence, allowing us to affirm his worth as a person and deal more rationally with the situation caused by the offence. 'A man's wisdom gives him patience; it is to his glory to overlook an offence' (Proverbs 19:11). There are many things that we could have a 'right' to get peeved about, but this verse tells us that wisdom gives patience. It is to our glory if we do not take offence, if we are forgiving in our attitude.

Consider a couple who, because of work and church commitments and the many incidentals of life, do not have much time alone together. One day the husband says, 'I'm going to be home on time tonight. I want you to be ready, and we'll go out for dinner alone, just the two of us. We're going to spend some quality time together, just to talk.'

As he walks out of the door, they are both eagerly anticipating the evening; she especially looks forward to it all day long as she cleans the house and does the ironing, and takes care of the children.

That night she gets everything ready; she gets the children to bed on time, arranges for a babyminder to come in, and dresses up in his favourite outfit. At six-thirty she has her coat, gloves and handbag on a chair by the door and is all ready to go. Six-thirty comes—and he is not there. Six-forty-five—he is late—again. This has happened before. He tries to keep his promises, but it does not always work out.

According to the rule laid out above, she now has a choice. Forgiveness involves separating the offence from the offender. It allows us to think positively about the person and deal more rationally with the situation. What is a rational attitude toward this offence? She is ready, and he is late. A rational attitude would say, 'What am I going to do with the time?' She could sit down and write some letters or read a good book (she probably has a lot of books that she is halfway through and would like to finish); she may have one or two pieces of sewing that she could do. She could do any of these things and use the time wisely, which would thereby enable her to keep the offence separate from her husband. After all, there are three considerations when things do not happen on time. First, we have wasted a certain portion of our life that could have been more effectively used if we had known exactly when things were going to happen. Second, the time we have for the activity may be shortened or, third, what we had planned may never happen at all. However, at this juncture the second two are hypothetical, and the first can be avoided.

On the other hand, she could develop a negative attitude, pace up and down and look out the window, glance at her watch, grumble and groan. In this heightened state of irritation, there is every chance that she will begin enumerating all his faults and will think the absolute worst about why he is late. She is also laying the groundwork for some hard work. The longer she frets, the more difficult it will be for her to forgive him once she realizes that this is what she must do, and there is a good chance that she will spoil the evening.

If we fail to separate the sin from the sinner and continue to identify the offence with the offender, bitterness will grow. Hurt and anger, if not taken care of immediately, tend to fester. The whole situation gets bigger, and bigger, and bigger.

Just a few years ago, something happened in our family. A friend hurt us in a way that I had never been hurt before. He hurt a member of our family who had gone through a lot already, and I have never felt so bad towards another

human being in all my life. The feelings were there in my
heart, very real feelings. Bad feelings can come, they exist
and we have to recognize that they are there. And believe
me, it helps to talk about them, to get them out in the open,
so that we can deal with them and Satan cannot build on
them.

This man had hurt me, hurt my family. I was having a
very hard time dealing with it, because I was being faced
with it every day. Oh, I knew all of this, and every time I
saw the man I was praying for him. I was praying very hard
for him, but I was not able to get on top of it, and it grew and
it grew and it grew—until I hated him. I had never hated
anybody in my life before; but I hated that man. It would
have suited me fine if he could have just died; I could have
rejoiced over it. I hated him so much. I believed the word,
when it says, 'Our hearts are deceitful and desperately
wicked.' I knew that, and I knew that any sin was possible,
because of my heart; but I had never hated anyone like that.
Every time I was filled with this emotion I would confess it
and ask the Lord to help me to have a right attitude about
this man. I had to do it over and over again. I did not feel
forgiveness, not one bit, because it was still there, and he
was still behaving in the same way. It was like pouring salt
over and over again into the wound. And I had to keep
giving this man to the Lord, and keep giving this situation
to the Lord, and keep giving my anger to the Lord, and keep
giving my hurt to the Lord.

It all came to a head when someone was giving a talk on
forgiveness during one Marriage Weekend. I was very
down on that particular Weekend, and during the talk, I
recognized where I was. I was very close to being enveloped
in bitterness and depression, because I was allowing this
man to rule in my life. All I could think about was what he
had done, what he had said, what he was doing. I was in
bondage, and could not get lose, but finally, on that Weekend I was able to get through to the Lord. I really and truly
gave it over to him and forgave that man with my will…and

was freed of him. The thing is still there; but I am free of it. Nothing will change the fact that this situation has taken place, but I am able to remember the offence without bitterly remembering the offender, and see the offender without bitterly remembering the offence.

Now I know that it is possible to forgive under some of the most extreme circumstances. I have forgiven, and I know peace in my heart. Emotions and feelings are real—I am not saying that they are not there. When they are there, we have to deal with them. But I know that when we allow bitterness to come in and build and build, and put its roots through our whole being, we are taken over. We cannot minister the love of God and contain bitterness at the same time.

To forgive, to separate the sin from the sinner, is a decision. A definite act of the will. To retain bitterness, and allow it to grow, is a decision, an act of the will. Much of the time it is an easier decision than the decision to forgive, just as spending money is easier than saving. But to decide to retain bitterness is like deciding to retain a cancer that could be removed.

Forgiveness places us in partnership with God to minister in the offender's life. Frequently an offence is simply a symptom of the offender's need. Forgiveness qualifies us to be in a position to minister to that need. Bitterness simply underlines the character deficiency. Recently we counselled a couple where the husband was very undisciplined and the wife was bitter about it and had a very negative spirit. The husband actually sat there and told Dave and me that he was undisciplined and could not be counted on to do anything. This went on and on for nearly an hour. He was very insensitive and completely lacking in compassion.

In the third session, we were thinking about financial mismanagement. The husband owned about six cars, and he was sharing his plan to sell some of them in order to clear all their debts, when the wife butted in and said, 'Well, what's the use? He'll only spend the money on something else, and we'll be in debt again.'

He *was* undisciplined, he *was* insensitive, he *was* selfish, and you might say she had a right to be bitter. But her bitterness underlined his faults to the point where he felt there was no hope for change. This can be a never-ending cycle: the offending partner wants to change, but the offended partner is so bitter that he or she just digs the rut deeper until the offender cannot crawl out. Bitterness disqualifies us from ministering.

Take the earlier illustration of the husband who came home late. It may have been insensitivity, and it may be that he was not only insensitive to her but was insensitive and hurtful to everyone. But in her bitterness she probably would not recognize this, any more than she would recognize where she herself was wrong. Forgiving him would make her able to pray for him, and she might even have an opportunity to speak to him about it. Then when she spoke to him about it, her words would not come from a person who was bitter and offended and just concerned about her own situation, but from a person who was not offended and not bitter, and who had an interest in his life. And aren't we all much more open to criticism from someone whose sole interest is to see us become better people?

Forgiveness is a decision and, like all decisions, it is based on faith: faith in the nature and character of God, as revealed in his word; faith that he will in fact empower us to do what he calls us to do. All faith decisions are tried and tested at one time or another, sometimes over and over again. There is a reason for this. Peter says that the trial of our faith is more precious than gold. God is not necessarily testing us for him to see if our faith is genuine, but for *us* to see that our faith is genuine, that the promises hold true, and that in him we do have the ability, in this instance, to forgive. One of the deep areas of hurt that we seem to be faced with over and over again, in marriage counselling, is the hurt that comes through adultery. Almost without exception, by the time a couple comes to us, the adultery is no longer the pertinent issue, but rather the offended party's inability to forgive.

In 1984, during the Mission England crusade at Ipswich, Richard and Donna came to Christ. Their marriage was in deep trouble. He had been unfaithful, and recognized that his life was becoming far too complicated. He had been invited to the Portman Road Stadium at the beginning of the Crusade, and under the ministry of Dr Graham was brought to a point of genuine repentance. He experienced tremendous excitement and freedom. When he shared with Donna his new-found joy and the forgiveness he had received from God, she realized that quite possibly this was what she, too, needed, and she went along to the Crusade and invited Christ into her life, also. She told the woman who was counselling her that they had serious marriage problems, and the woman, who was a member of our church, spotted Dave out on the field and introduced him to Donna.

They came along for counselling a week or so later. He was exuberant in his new-found faith and excited about all that Jesus was doing in his life. He was into the word, was sharing the gospel, and having a wonderful prayer life. But Donna was down in the pits. It took several sessions to deal with all the issues that were woven into this, but the main thrust was her inability to forgive. At first it seemed absolutely impossible, she had been hurt far too deeply. Their sex life was absolutely nil. Her thoughts were trapped in a treadmill: an arm around the shoulder reminded her of intimacy, intimacy reminded her of sex, sex reminded her of adultery, adultery reminded her of the other woman— whom she knew. And to make matters worse, here was Richard, the offender, just bubbling over, like so many new converts; she was deeply miserable.

Almost all of Donna's homework assignments following the counselling sessions were geared towards helping her to understand the spiritual dynamics of forgiveness: the fact that it was non-optional, the fact that it was a decision, and the fact that God would certainly empower her to make that decision and maintain it. God finally got through to her. She was able to forgive this woman from her heart, and Richard as well. And every facet of their marriage began to improve. Her spiritual life began to improve, too. She became more and more active and outspoken in their nurture group, which by now had continued on into a growth group. She had finally entered into the victory of her salvation.

However, it was not an 'out of sight, out of mind' situation. The other woman was miserable. Life was becoming far too complex for her to deal with, too. Their circles of acquaintances were interwoven so that this woman, Joanne, continued to hear reports. First she heard that Richard and Donna were 'religious', and then that they had 'gone off their rocker'. After that the stories settled down to reports about how much they had changed. One of the complicating factors in Joanne's life was a tremendous weight of guilt, and the guilt increased in proportion to the changes that were taking place in Richard and Donna.

She wrote a letter to Donna, asking her forgiveness. Donna wrote back telling her that she had forgiven her. Then Joanne sent another letter in which she talked about the change in their lives and the fact that she was searching, and that she would like to meet Donna. This was a real test for Donna, and she really did not know how she should react. Unfortunately, many of their Christian friends were advising against a meeting. They said that she had a responsibility to forgive, but was under no obligation to form a relationship with this woman who had caused so much pain in her life.

Richard phoned us to ask how we viewed the situation. At first, it seemed like one more of those times when we wished people did not value our opinion, because we would rather not give one. It is not very logical to advise a woman who has had such a difficulty with forgiveness to open the door to a relationship with the very person who has offended against her. But then the light dawned, and we said, 'God wants to show you something very special: he wants to show you how powerful he is, how great his resources are to overcome bitterness, and how much he has done in your life. This woman is hurting, and is searching for what you have. You can fulfil a function that no priest or pastor could ever do because you have the most accurate, up-to-date portrayal of the gospel of anyone on the face of the earth.'

It is one thing to be a Good Samaritan; but how much more powerful is a person who has been personally offended yet is able to minister to the offender. This is the epitome of a changed life. And so Donna reached out to Joanne. She was able to share the gospel with her and help her get established in a church in her own town. Forgiveness places us in partnership with God to minister in the offender's life.

The consequences of bitterness

The consequences of bitterness are spiritual, psychological and physical. I have already outlined the spiritual consequences of bitterness. When we do not forgive, we violate God's law and consequently are out of fellowship with him. We lack power in our life. We frequently hear people say, 'I don't feel that my prayers are getting any higher than the ceiling. The heavens have turned to brass.' Frequently this is due to unforgiveness: 'And when you stand praying, if you hold anything against anyone, forgive him, so that your Father in heaven may forgive you your sins' (Mark 11:25). Jesus is saying that if we want answers to our prayers, if we want action, we have got to be in fellowship with him. Possibly we need to look around and see if there is anyone towards whom we are holding a bitter spirit. If there is, we need to forgive them quickly if we want our prayers answered.

The emotional consequences of bitterness are devastating, too. Holding a grudge is an emotional drain which saps a lot of mental energy, which in turn leads to depression.

Frequently we hold a grudge against another person because of something he has done, and he may not even know it. He goes off scot-free, and we are the only ones who are hurt. We are the ones who are being punished, not the other person. Not being able to forgive others can turn our thoughts inward to an unhealthy state, and I certainly did find this was true when I was going through my battle with bitterness. I became depressed and was unable to think clearly on any subject.

A tremendous amount of research still needs to be done on the physical consequences of bitterness. Medical people cannot make scientifically verifiable statements which categorically link bitterness with physical manifestations. However, most of this inability to make categorical statements comes down to the fact that these things are difficult to measure because there is no such thing as a 'standard' or 'normal' physical body. Because bodies vary, it is impossible to say that this or that physical breakdown was caused by bitterness. However, there are many scientifically verifiable facts which prove that mental stress and tension contribute to physical breakdown. And bitterness is a state of mental stress and tension.

For instance, it has been scientifically demonstrated that when the body is under stress it has a decreased ability to produce the protective mucous lining of the stomach. The stomach contains gastric juices which are very strong acids and can dissolve almost anything which acids normally act on. Consequently, if the protective mucous lining is removed, the gastric juices begin to digest the stomach itself. When the gastric juices begin to affect the lining of the stomach, this creates an ulcer. Therefore, having an ulcer is a tension-related disease. It is possible to have an ulcer without tension, because it is possible that the body's ability to produce this mucous lining may be lowered for other reasons. However, since ulcers seem to occur most frequently amongst people under tension, and we know that tension lowers the body's ability to produce this lining, it is not wrong to assume that when people under tension get ulcers, there is a direct causal link.

This type of breakdown is observable in many parts of the body. In his book *None of These Diseases* (Marshall Pickering) Dr S. I. Macmillan states, 'Verbal expression of animosity towards others calls for a certain hormone from the pituitary, adrenal, thyroid and other glands, an excess of which can cause disease in any part of the body.'

Obviously the tension caused by bitterness produces a chemical change within the body, and this will manifest itself at the weakest point, not always causing disease, but accelerating physical breakdown. We heard on the news recently that two people were being tried for manslaughter because they had knowingly angered a man who had recently had heart surgery. We do not know what the outcome was, but it is very significant that a lawyer considered that he could base such a case on the relationship between emotion and physical breakdown. Unforgiveness could drastically shorten our life-span.

The results of unforgiveness can even be passed on from one generation to the next, 'visiting the iniquity of the fathers upon the children unto the third and fourth generation of them that hate me' (Deut 5:9b, AV).

We had one very sad letter in response to our survey. It came from a woman who felt it was futile to fill in the survey sheet. She wrote, 'When we attended the Christian Marriage Weekend, I was feeling pretty depressed about our marriage, and still am. We have been married over forty years, and I have four children and nine grandchildren. We both profess to be Christians, though our children have rejected Christianity. We have not found marriage easy, and the course made us realize just how little we communicated and just how many grudges we hold against each other.' It would seem fairly obvious from the statement 'many grudges we hold against each other', that Christianity was professed in this home, but not lived out. This certainly gave an opportunity for the children to say in their hearts,

'If this is Christianity, I do not want it.' The really sad thing in this marriage is that after having been faced with the truth, they refused to do anything about it. It is never too late to change. The iniquities of the parents do not have to be visited upon the children. All that is necessary to break the cycle is to forgive and to throw ourselves on God's mercy for the strength to do so. Deuteronomy 5:10, following on from that reference to the iniquities of the parents, states, 'And shewing mercy unto thousands of them that love me and keep my commandments.'

Overcoming the inertia of bitterness

'Forgiving and forgetting' is a cliché we often hear. It is mistakenly based on God's promise that he 'will remember our sins no more'. However, this is an obvious literary form used to convey a principle about God's forgiveness, and is not to be taken literally. I always wince when I say the words, 'not to be taken literally', but the fact is that there are many such literary statements in the Bible which, if taken literally, would contradict many truths about God. It is totally illogical to think that the God who knows everything would not know something that we know. We know a woman who is an ex-prostitute and drug addict, and she has a ministry in many parts of the world which involves sharing her testimony with thousands of people. Hence, there are thousands and thousands of people who know of her prostitution, and probably hundreds who know of it first-hand. It is unreasonable to think that God does not know this.

In some US Government agencies where it is hard to dismiss employees, they begin an 'unfavourable information folder' on a problem employee, and file each misdemeanour in this folder until enough information is amassed to justify the employee's dismissal. God's statement, 'I will remember your sins no more', simply means that God does not maintain an unfavourable information folder on anything that we have confessed and he has forgiven. Forgiveness is tearing up unfavourable information folders. The information may be stored elsewhere in our minds as a fact of life, but we must get rid of the folder.

The law of inertia states that a moving object tends to stay in motion, and a stationary object tends to stay stationary. If bitterness has been around for a while, we have a tendency to feel it cannot be moved. The following are some steps to help overcome this inertia.

1. Admit to bitterness. If we feel upset whenever we think of a certain situation, incident or individual, we are bitter. We listened to a man recently tell us for the fifth time how he had been mistreated in a certain church. He claimed to have forgiven the individuals involved, but as he told the story his voice began to rise and his frustration level mounted to the extent that he could scarcely even carry on a conversation after he had finished. All he could do was wave his hands and say, 'Where do I go from here?' He was still bitter.

2. List the problem areas where God is working in your life: things like laziness, rebellion, lack of discipline, insensitivity.

3. Reconsider each situation that is causing you bitterness in the light of Romans 8:29 (God is conforming us to the likeness of his Son). Frequently God allows unpleasant instances to crop up in order to work on some of our negative qualities. Our question should not be, 'Why has this happened, Lord?' but, 'What are you trying to teach me, Lord?'

4. Reflect on the amount of forgiveness your own actions have required from God and others on your life-journey, and remember the parable of the unforgiving servant.

5. Consider the consequences of bitterness: that bitterness can shorten your life, impair your mental functions, and, worst of all, take you out of fellowship with God. It is a luxury you cannot afford.

6. Make a commitment to forgive the offender, never to

use the incident against him, to separate the sin from the sinner. If it helps, write out the offence on a piece of paper, fold it in half, label it, 'So-and-so's unfavourable information folder', and then throw it in the fireplace.

7. Look for ways to demonstrate your new attitude. Doris Westbrook tells of an instance where a teacher on her staff had offended her. Doris had forgiven her, but still the relationship was strained. Doris was asking the Lord for a special way to demonstrate her attitude of forgiveness. When she heard that this teacher was going to have a group of visiting football players in her home for the weekend, she baked a pie and took it around to the teacher's house and told her she thought she could use it with all those hungry boys in the house for the weekend. It brought tears to the other woman's eyes, and it certainly conveyed an attitude of forgiveness and restored the relationship completely.

For further consideration

Remember, if I have lost my inner peace, it is not because someone has sinned against me. A lack of peace shows that I have reacted wrongly, and the name of my sin is unforgiveness.

Are we keeping any 'unfavourable information folders' against anyone? Have we really forgiven?

Chapter 12

Our Birthright—Transparency

'The wrath of God is being revealed from heaven against all the godlessness and wickedness of men who suppress the truth by their wickedness, since what may be known about God is plain to them, because God has made it plain to them' (Rom 1:18–19).

Godless men deal with sin in two ways: they attempt either to hide it or to normalize it. Hiding sin is to suppress the truth about our own actions. Normalizing sin is to suppress the truth about God's standards.

When Adam and Eve sinned, they hid from God. But hiding from God was not enough; they even had to hide from each other. They had eaten from the tree of knowledge of good and evil, and not only had they gained the knowledge of good and evil, as manifested by their guilt, but they evidently gained an exaggerated sense of good and evil, because they perceived even their differences to be evil. Consequently, they used their human ingenuity to sew together fig leaves and cover themselves. They could no longer stand to be naked: nakedness represented vulnerability. Fallen mankind has had a difficult time with vulnerability ever since. True, some have learned to be comfortable in nudist colonies; but psychological nakedness and vulnerability is another question.

Normalizing sin, the second mode of dealing with it, began in the Garden of Eden. Satan's comment, 'Hath God said...?' was designed to suppress the truth of God's standards. It began in the Garden of Eden; but I do not think it came into full blossom until the twentieth century. We live in an age of normalizing sin. Few people hide their abuses; in fact, they even flaunt them. Fifty years ago the idea of unmarried couples living together was an absolute anathema. Today, in some circles, it is much more in vogue than being married. Normalizing sin is saying, 'Yes, I do it—but it's perfectly normal. There's nothing wrong in it.'

The proper way of handling sin is to confess it: 'If we confess our sins, he is faithful and just and will forgive us our sins and purify us from all unrighteousness' (1 John 1:9). To confess a sin means to name the act and call it what God calls it—sin. People who normalize sin are confessing it, but they are not calling it sin, and they do not have the blood of Jesus Christ to cleanse them. Consequently, their confession is like writing a cheque with no money in the bank. Transparency is every Christian's birthright, bought and paid for by the Lord Jesus Christ. The necessary capital is in the bank to cover all our sins. By confessing it, we draw on that account.

Maintaining a clear conscience through a vertical relationship with God does not in itself provide the necessary transparency because this does not fulfil all God's requirements. In chapter 5, we discussed the fact that Christianity is lived out through our relationships with others. God requires us to clear our conscience with one another as well as with him. When I, Dave, go to God and confess how thoughtless I have been to Joyce, I hear him say, if I listen carefully, 'You've told me—now go tell Joyce.' In other words, confessing sins that involve other individuals is only a part of the solution, only a part of the process of gaining a clear conscience. 'Leave your gift there in front of the altar. First go and be reconciled to your brother; then come and offer your gift' (Matt 5:24). We are commanded to put things right with our brother on the horizontal, as well as with God on the vertical.

If we fail in either dimension, we find that we are hanging little fig leaves here and there on our life. If we hang fig leaves, we cannot walk out in a breeze for fear of our sin being revealed. We live in a constant state of fear that we will be discovered. 'The wicked man flees though no-one pursues, but the righteous are as bold as a lion' (Prov 28:1).

On the other hand, if, as Christians, we attempt to normalize our sin, it strains our relationship with other believers whom we know would not agree with our 'new perspective'.

A girl we once knew went to another town to have an abortion. None of her Christian friends knew that she was pregnant or even involved in such a relationship. They knew where she was, but they did not know why she went and they thought it peculiar when she would not respond to any attempts to contact her. The fact was that she had normalized her situation to herself, and she knew that if she faced her friends she would be forced either to hide the situation or attempt to 'convert' them. She realized this was impossible, because she had not really convinced herself, but by staying away from her Christian fellowship, she could avoid her guilt (at least temporarily).

Proper handling of sin yields a clear conscience, which in turn allows us to be transparent towards everyone. It gives us the freedom to be ourselves. With a clear conscience, we no longer view our differences from others as wrong. We are much less prone to see righteousness as conforming to a group, and we are able to be completely transparent, which is every Christian's birthright.

The Bible views a clear conscience as indispensable equipment: 'Timothy, my son, I give you this instruction in keeping with the prophecies once made about you, so that by following them you may fight the good fight, holding on to faith and a good conscience. Some have rejected these and so have shipwrecked their faith' (1 Tim 1:18–19). Paul saw a clear conscience as a weapon in fighting the good fight.

Peter saw it as equally important: 'But in your hearts set apart Christ as Lord. Always be prepared to give an answer to everyone who asks you to give the reason for the hope that you have. But do this with gentleness and respect, keeping a clear conscience, so that those who speak maliciously against your good behaviour in Christ may be ashamed of their slander' (1 Pet 3:15–16).

There are times when we become acutely aware of the state of our conscience: in prayer, at the Lord's Supper, and when we are performing some aspect of ministry. However, I am convinced that there is no time when we are more sensitive to the state of our conscience than when we are about to witness for Christ. Lack of skill, unfamiliarity with the Scriptures and inexperience are deterrents to witnessing, but I feel that these are dwarfed by the main deterrent, which is the lack of a clear conscience—exactly the point that both Peter and Paul are making.

During my last few years in the Air Force my witnessing had to take on a different style. It is unethical to witness to people who feel themselves obliged to listen to you because of your position, so I hung a sign on my wall that simply said, 'Have Jesus—will share'. It worked rather well. It caused people to ask questions, and it was decidedly more effective to answer questions that people were asking than answer questions that no one was asking. But the moment I put up the sign, I became the resident 'Jesus freak'. People were examining my life; my boss compared me with every other manager who had ever worked for him; my subordinates compared me with every other boss they ever had; the way I shined my shoes, kept my car, spent my time, etc, was always under scrutiny.

In that office we had a secretary who was a notorious purveyor of gossip, which created immense problems among the personnel. One day a young woman on our staff came to me in tears as a result of something said by this secretary. I had already given several warnings, and now I wrote the secretary a formal letter of counselling, which was a fairly serious disciplinary action. Her husband worked in one of the fighter squadrons, and one day he was invited by a member of his squadron to attend a chapel luncheon for men. He said, 'Will Dave Ames be there?' The other fellow assured him that I would. He said, 'Well, then I don't want to go. That Dave Ames calls himself a Christian, but you should see the way he treats the people that work for him.'

The following month one of my most dependable men overslept on a morning when he was supposed to open the office early. A very important executive was scheduled to be there at the same time, and was kept waiting for about twenty minutes. My commander and the executive officer were both very embarrassed over the situation and wanted to 'throw the book' at this young man. But it was up to me to initiate the action. After half an hour, my argument that his record did not justify such stern treatment eventually stood against all their objections, and their final parting shot to me was, 'Come on, Ames, you can't save everybody.'

This is exactly what Peter was talking about: people will speak maliciously against our good behaviour. On the one hand, I was portrayed as Captain Blythe—'That Dave Ames calls himself a Christian, but you should see how he treats his people'—and on the other hand as a person who would not take proper disciplinary action because he was a Christian. People will speak maliciously against even our good behaviour, and we do not dare give them the least bit of 'real' ammunition. We know this, and this is why we are loath to witness in a lot of places. We know that when we identify ourselves as Christians, someone may say, 'You call yourself a Christian—and I have to do half your work?' or, 'You call yourself a Christian, and you tell the kind of jokes you do?' etc.

The lack of a clear conscience even affects us physically. 'Blessed is he whose transgressions are forgiven, whose sins are covered. Blessed is the man whose sin the Lord does not count against him and in whose spirit is no deceit. When I kept silent, my bones wasted away through my groaning all day long. For day and night your hand was heavy upon me; my strength was sapped as the heat of summer' (Ps 32:1–4).

A young man who was about to be discharged from the Air Force came to me with a problem so grave that he felt that his life was falling apart. Before coming to Christ, he had been a homosexual. As he was sharing his problem with me, we were riding in a car through Mildenhall airbase. Just as we passed his old barracks, he was explaining the magnitude of his involvement. He pointed to the barracks and said that at one time he had had an affair with every man who lived in that barracks. When he came to Christ he was completely freed from this. He went home on leave and met a girl with whom he fell deeply in love. He later proposed to her by letter. He knew it would be wise to tell her about his past, but he did not think it was good to do so through correspondence. The next time he went home, she shared with him that when she was a little girl she had been accosted by a lesbian, and she thought homosexuality was the most repulsive sin in the catalogue. Needless to say, he lost his courage to share his past with her. He vowed he would do it when he came back for their wedding; but he did not, because he was afraid their wedding would never take place if he did, and this was the first meaningful relationship he had ever had. He brought her back to England, and then lived in constant fear that someone who knew his past would inform his wife. His job involved an extremely high security clearance. He began to develop stomach problems and general nervousness; the doctors immediately recognized that this was more than a physical problem, and sent him to the mental health clinic. The mental health clinic withdrew his security clearance, which reduced him to being clerk-typist in the administrative section. His condition deteriorated. He was given a psychiatric diagnosis and recommended for discharge. When he came to me, he was at his wit's end, and said, 'I just know I'll lose my wife and little baby. The thought is tearing me apart.'

I then made him realize that not all his problems were because of his past, but because his conscience was not clear, and that if he kept on his present course he would surely lose his wife and baby, if for no other reason than that he lacked the ability to support them. We went through many scriptures together and claimed many promises, and prayed fervently; and he shared with his wife. And this lovely Christian girl forgave him. The last letter I had from them said that he had a job and they were established in a church. So much of the power of a guilty conscience is really only bluff: 'The wicked man flees though *no-one* pursues, but the righteous are as bold as a lion' (Prov 28:1, italics added).

'He who conceals his sins does not prosper, but whoever confesses and renounces them finds mercy' (Prov 28:13). We do not prosper because we lack the transparency that is generated by a clear conscience. Vulnerability is highly attractive, because there is no vulnerability without trust; and people who are trusting are deemed to be trustworthy, and people who are trustworthy are much more apt to be successful. Consequently, it is a demonstrable fact of life that 'he who conceals his sin does not prosper'.

Why are so many so prone to procrastinate when it comes to taking action to clear their conscience? Well, obviously, it takes courage. This lack of courage inspires some very creative rationalization to avoid taking the steps to clear our conscience. I think it would be good to take a look at a few of the more common rationalizations, just to put them in perspective.

● 'It was such a long time ago.' Not so long ago that you cannot remember, and your conscience is still bothering you. The other person probably remembers it, as well.

● 'Things are better now.' It may simply be that God is preparing the way for us to put things right without a blow-up. Emotional fire is out of the situation, which will

157

enable us to discuss things rationally.

● 'Admitting my guilt will make me financially liable.' Better a clear conscience with an honest debt, than living with a guilty conscience. Remember, it is God who is convicting you, and it is God who is interested in clearing your conscience; and he owns the cattle on a thousand hills.

● 'The other person was the main offender.' The fact that we may be able to prove that the other person was ninety per cent wrong, does not relieve us from our ten per cent of guilt. God is not holding us responsible for the other person's behaviour, but our own. It may well be that confessing our responsibility will enable the other person to confess theirs, and the entire relationship will be restored.

● 'This is a "besetting sin". I would spend half my life confessing.' Sometimes God performs inexplicable miracles in changing our lives; at other times, he uses more observable dynamics. If we really humble ourselves to go and put things right, we will think twice before we commit the same sin again. And after we have done this a few times, because we have learned the value of a clear conscience, we will begin to gain almost miraculous control of the areas that we had once thought were hopeless.

● 'It should be sufficient to commit myself to change in this area.' That is a good start; but there are two problems. One is that there is still a barrier between myself and a brother. And the other is that, without some declaration on my part, the offended party has no way of knowing that that is not my normal behaviour. Supposing I borrow a tool and bring it back in a very abused condition; I borrow a chisel and accidentally hit a nail and put a big chip in it. If I simply return it with no comment, how is the other person to know that is not the way I normally handle tools? On the other hand, if I explain and offer to pay for it, they may say something like, 'That's all right, this was not one of the good ones. Don't worry about it.' But the next time I come to borrow a tool, they will know I appreciate tools and intend to act responsibly. If I say nothing, they have no way of knowing what my idea of responsibility is.

● 'The offended party is not a Christian. It would be a poor testimony.' On the contrary, it may be a wonderful testimony. We know, as Christians, that we are not perfect, and the world also knows that Christians are not perfect. Unfortunately, the world often thinks that we think we *are* perfect. This may be a wonderful opportunity to explain what the gospel is all about.

Gaining a clear conscience

To gain a clear conscience, we need to take an inventory. This is something the world cannot afford to do; the world calls it 'introspection'. Introspection is different from an inventory. Introspection is taking an inventory with no hope of being able to make up the losses. We have hope. I need to ask myself questions like:

● Have I stolen anything from anyone? From shops, friends, family? Allowed myself unauthorized 'perks' at the office?

● Have I failed to tell the truth? Have I deliberately lied to cover myself, or failed to give facts that might reflect unfavourably on me?

● Have I acted in rage? I may have been speaking the truth, but it may not have been in love.

● Have I been guilty of gossiping about others? It is very tempting to pass on the latest exploits of someone who is not very popular. Comments made about them make everyone feel justified in their opinion and put us in the 'in circle'.

● Have I had a problem with my attitudes? Have I failed to show appreciation properly for the sacrifices of others? Have I been rebellious, lazy or insensitive? All of these things build barriers between us and others.

When we apologize, we must work out the wording in advance. The prodigal son did this: 'Father, I have sinned against heaven and against you. I am no longer worthy to be called your son; make me like one of your hired men'

(Luke 15:18b—19). We can say a lot of things that are ineffective and even compound matters if we do not take precautions in advance. This step in the process should not be avoided. It is a way of making sure that our heartfelt attitude is properly conveyed to the other individual.

Let us look at some of the things that are ineffective:

● 'If I've been wrong....' This quite naturally does not say a thing, because it simply does not assume responsibility for anything; and yet we hear it so often.

● 'I know we were both wrong....' This goes a small step further because it assumes a little responsibility; but it could be disastrous, because it places responsibility on someone else who may not feel they have any responsibility in the issue at all.

● 'I'm sorry about it, but part of the problem is....' And then we go on to share the guilt with two or three others. This is slightly better, but confessions should be about our own guilt. James 5:16 tells us to confess our sins to each other—not other people's sins.

There are three important elements in asking forgiveness: First an admission of guilt; second, a statement of the offence; and third, a clear-cut request for forgiveness. For example:

●'I was wrong.' (The three hardest words in the English language to link together.)

● 'The way I spoke was very rude.' (This identifies the basic offence—rudeness.)

● 'Will you forgive me?' (This is a clear-cut statement which requires a response from the other individual.)

Some say that if we are the offending party, it is wrong for us to manipulate the other person into a position which requires an answer from them. But the contrary is true: because we are the offending party we have a responsibility to set up a situation which makes it as easy as possible for our brother to forgive us, so that he can avoid the pitfall of bitterness.

Some very important considerations must be borne in

mind when clearing our conscience. Not only must our words be concise, but our attitude must be right. We do not dare just pop in on someone with a prearranged formula and expect them to be able to react from their heart. We should pray in advance and ask the Lord to show us exactly what it is going to cost this other person to forgive us. God approves of a broken spirit and a contrite heart, and so do others.

Select the proper time and place. Consider the opportunity for privacy and the other person's mood. On the whole, a personal visit is better than a phone call, but a phone call may be necessary. Generally speaking, we should 'go' to them, as Scripture demands.

A lot of marriage relationships are clouded, and sex lives tarnished, because of premarital sexual relations. It is important that marriage partners who have had this problem should ask each other's forgiveness and take it before God and ask him to cleanse their relationship from this violation of his law. This may at first present a problem with wording, in view of the instructions a few paragraphs back about not sharing the guilt, but something like, 'God has convicted me of the fact that I took advantage of our relationship. Will you forgive me?' works quite nicely. An appropriate response when asked for forgiveness is never, 'That's all right, I was wrong, too.' It should always be to say, 'Yes, I forgive you,' and then to confess your own responsibility.

One last and very important consideration is the issue of adultery. It is not good for one partner to tip all his rubbish on another in order to gain a clear conscience. On our second Marriage Weekend, we had a fighter pilot confess multiple episodes of adultery to his wife, who was devastated. She finally came through it, and their marriage is stronger for it now, but I am afraid she would not be a strong advocate of Marriage Weekends. From that time on we have strongly recommended that, with this particular issue or something of this magnitude, the offending party confess it to someone whom they consider to be an elder;

and if a woman find another women of the calibre of an elder to share it with. The person to whom they are confessing should know both the husband and the wife well enough to be able to advise whether the time is right to share this with the partner. We have frequently seen situations where the advice was, 'Not now.' In one situation, it took two years before the time was right. There is a reason for doing this. First, we have taken all the steps advisable to put the situation right, even to the point of making ourselves vulnerable to another human being. This is evidence of our repentance and commitment, and gives us a clear conscience. Secondly, should the offended party learn of the situation before the confession is made to them, there is a record of our right intentions.

It is not unreasonable to expect that when we make the effort to put something right with an individual who may be equally wrong, they may want to confess their responsibility. However, it is wrong to go into a situation expecting this, because it may not happen. We cannot use our apology to manipulate another individual into apologizing; it is only to clear our conscience. A clear conscience towards God and our fellow man means that no one can point a finger at us over past wrongs that have never been put right.

'The wicked man flees though no-one pursues, but the righteous are as bold as a lion' (Prov 28:1).

For further consideration

Discuss the correlation betweeen a clear conscience and the ability to have effective feeling-level communication.

Chapter 13

Relating to God through Prayer

It may seem peculiar in a book dealing with marriage, to start this chapter by emphasizing a solitary activity: that of personal prayer and devotion, especially since the main thrust of this chapter is praying together as couples. However, we are following the priorities that we have already discussed. Our relationship with God is a personal relationship, a relationship which is basically one-to-one: God and us. When we stand before God on that final day, it will be as individuals, not as a couple. Our function in that relationship will certainly be addressed, but the topic will always be individual responsibility. Consequently, each day there must be a personal, private time alone with God where we discuss our journey as an individual.

Even the most dedicated, totally involved couples recognize that this involvement has individual responsibility. For instance, when we are preparing for a Marriage Weekend or a conference, or any speaking engagement where we are going to speak together as a couple, we spend a lot of time together 'brainstorming', jotting down ideas; but we always wind up the sessions by assigning individual responsibility for each part of the programme. Then we spend a certain amount of time alone in preparation. We generally come back together to 'bounce around' the ideas

that we have come up with; but there is individual preparation because there is individual responsibility. When we
stand up to speak, we alternate back and forth. Even if we
stand together arm-in-arm and speak alternate paragraphs,
what is said still comes out of one mouth or the other, and
therefore must be completely thought out in advance by the
partner who is speaking.

With God, there is an even more important issue at stake,
which is the fact that his first priority in our life is to
conform us to the image of his Son. Because of this, there
are questions in our mind when we hear couples claim to do
everything together, including *all* their devotions. It is
wonderful for a husband and wife to have a devotional time
together. But time alone with God must be exactly that:
alone. To avoid this is to avoid our responsibility to our
relationship with God as individuals, which must take
precedence over everything else.

Having established individual responsibility, we want to
move on to a very important facet of married life—praying
as a couple. Couples' prayer is a very important concept
because it is a way of underlining the priority of our
relationship. In our time alone with God we bring ourselves
before God and discuss our personal journey. Through
couples' prayer we bring our marriage relationship before
God and talk to him about our progress, our fears, our joys,
our desires and our concerns.

The feedback we get through our critique sheets and
surveys tells us that many couples have very little experience
in this area before attending a Marriage Weekend. Some in
fact, have never prayed together prior to a Marriage Weekend. Marriage Weekends prove to be an ideal place to
develop this ability for a very simple reason that we ourselves
had never considered until we began writing this book. We
ask couples to pray in their rooms after each communication
session. Each of these sessions follows a talk on one particular topic: priorities, finances, forgiveness, etc. So each
time the couples pray, it only involves a simple prayer over

a 'single-stranded issue'. Couples who have never prayed together before find it easy to pray a short prayer about their new insight on priorities or finances. Presumably most of them pray together like this eight or nine times over the weekend. This in turn makes it much less difficult to pray about two or three issues on Monday, after the Weekend is over.

This type of 'follow-up' to a Marriage Weekend is the most important single factor in enabling the 'new beginnings' of a Marriage Weekend to continue. It is both effective and biblical, and it honours God as the third partner in the marriage relationship. On some Marriage Weekends they suggest that couples spend ten minutes or so a day writing a thought to their partner, and then ten more minutes a day discussing the thought. This is certainly a helpful device in stimulating communication, and it is something that we highly recommend if couples find that things are going unsaid for one reason or another. However, it comes a poor second to an effective prayer time together as a couple. Over the years we have been only too well aware that busy couples, especially those with small children, have difficulty in establishing a daily routine which will insure ten or fifteen minutes together each day at a given time. To be realistic, it is very much an either-or situation: either a couple has time to establish the discipline of writing notes and discussing them, or they have time to pray together. So since there is a high probability that a couple will only do one or the other, we feel that we must invest our encouragement in couples' prayer. We realize that if ten or fifteen minutes alone is all a couple gets every day, then they have problems. Most couples have more, but the amount that they have over that is, first of all, not always predictable, and secondly, it comes at a time not conducive to practising a discipline. Sometimes it is not until nine o'clock at night, when they both want to flop down with a hot drink and just talk.

Praying as a couple is a very unifying activity. Just as

praying together as a church unifies a church, praying together as a couple unifies a couple. Many pastors consider the mid-week prayer meeting to be the most important service of all. The primary reason for this is that it brings the needs of the church before the Lord. But there is an important secondary reason, and that is that it unifies the faithful into an effective solidarity. We see the same principle even more clearly demonstrated in house-groups. In fact, it may be reasonable to say that the smaller the group, the more unifying prayer together can become.

When we were children, most of us at one time or another experienced a situation where adults were talking about very important issues and we were asked to leave the room. The sense of exclusion that we then felt can keep coming back to us throughout life, since at one time or another we are not allowed to be privy to significant discussions which are limited to those with a 'need to know'. Sadly, many a wife is made to feel she is a junior partner, first because her husband keeps her in the dark about the decision-making process, and, second, because he does not really want her around when he is talking to God about it, either.

Roy and Diane had been married for thirty-six years when they came on a Marriage Weekend. They were committed Christians of long standing and highly respected pillars of their church. He was a deacon and definitely the leader in the home, although he had a tendency to be the 'strong, silent type'. Diane was the more verbal of the two and much more nearly fit the 'little woman at home' type.

Several areas of the Marriage Weekend benefited them. In fact, they are two of the greatest proponents of Christian Marriage Weekends that we know. However, the most important single item that they took home from the Marriage Weekend was prayer. Although Roy was a deacon he was, as we have said, the silent type. He had seldom prayed publicly in his life, and they had never prayed together as a husband and wife in their entire thirty-six years of marriage. She definitely felt very much like a junior partner. In fact, she said she felt her opinions just did not count. This single item revolutionized their lives.

The change began on the Marriage Weekend, when we saw them walking around hand-in-hand like a couple of teenagers. They began to feel closer together than they ever had been. We need to emphasize again that they had a very good marriage before they came. They had done an outstanding job of raising children, they were well respected in the community, and no one could have faulted their marriage. But praying together made them realize how important they were to each other. And this personal significance began to manifest itself even outside the relationship. Diane, this 'little woman at home', became a very dynamic, outspoken organizer who was able to take on the chairmanship of the ladies' work at one of the busiest Mission England areas in East Anglia.

One day, when she stepped down off the platform after speaking to six hundred ladies, she came over and kissed both of us and told us it would not have been possible except for 'what happened on the Marriage Weekend'. And what happened on the Marriage Weekend was that they began to pray together. Naturally we would like to tell you that it was some brilliant talk that we gave, or some creative insight that they had gained from us, but it was not anything like that. They simply began to pray together as a couple, after thirty-six years of dodging the issue.

The first thing that is necessary is to establish the priority of prayer, the fact that we really need to pray together as a couple. The next thing is to establish a specific time and place. No one can do this for us because we all have different schedules. Our time is first thing in the morning, with a mug full of tea, up in our bedroom, usually still in our pyjamas. And we do not make heavy going of it. It is not the time we pray for the Queen and the President of the United States. It is a time when we pray about ourselves and our kids, our parents and our ministry, the people we are going to counsel that day, and maybe one or two other issues of immediate concern. It is not a time to be long winded or to impress one another with our use of the language of Zion. The important thing is that there is a routine.

Don and Martha came on a Weekend over three years ago knowing they had certain areas in their marriage that could use improvement, mainly in communication. They had prayed together on odd occasions before coming on the Weekend, and although they could scarcely remember any particular item that had made a difference in their marriage, they claimed over a 60% improvement in their marriage as a result of praying together. It did not all happen right away, but they left the Weekend knowing that this was what they had to do. With three teenage children, they at first found it difficult to establish a routine, but eventually they did, and their marriage relationship has continued to deepen and improve over the past three years. They attribute all this improvement to one thing—praying together as a couple.

We are frequently asked about family devotions, which would be the next thing up the priority scale. We have to admit that this is an area where we do not have much first-hand information because we were unsuccessful in establishing a routine when our children were growing up. However, we attribute our failure to the very common practice of trying to do too much. Many families attempt to have a mini-church service, which is usually too long and too formal for children. Families we have seen that have been most successful simply read a passage of Scripture after the evening meal and then ask for comments on it, following this with a short time of prayer. The responsibility for 'leading' this devotion time can be passed around to different family members so that each person in turn reads the passage for the evening and asks a question. The evening meal makes a good time for this because the whole family is usually together. The practice should not be interrupted just because guests are invited. The key is not to make it heavy going, but to keep it simple. The more complex the process, the less chance it has of success.

Family devotions are important, but couples' prayer is more important. It might be fair to say it is the foundation for family devotions. In fact, it may be reasonable to say there is a second reason why our family devotions were not successful, and that is the fact that we were not praying together regularly as a couple at that time. Family devotions is not an easy thing to start, nor is it an easy thing to maintain, but it is well worth the effort.

For further consideration

Discuss how you might begin a simple prayer life together, or what changes might need to be made.

Discuss making a commitment to be growing Christians and to share this growth through prayer together as a couple.

Consider the relationship between openness with each other and the potential for real maturity of character as Christians.

Chapter 14

Meeting Needs

The differences between men and women laid out in chapters 6, 7 and 9, not only lay a logical foundation for family roles, but also pave the way for understanding certain idiosyncrasies that must be taken into consideration in meeting needs.

A husband who is busy single-strandedly working through the logic of a house purchase in the left side of his brain, is apt to reject out of hand his wife's intuitive reasoning that this is not a 'good deal'. This would, of course, be poor stewardship because he is ignoring the data which comes from a 'computer' capable of global reasoning, in favour of his own single-stranded logic, without attempting to take advantage of both. Not only is it poor stewardship, but it is also rejection. And as such, it represents a failure on his part to affirm her worth as a person. This frequent and frustrating manifestation of the difference between men and women can be used as an opportunity to show love.

Through patient probing, the husband can usually begin to isolate certain issues within his wife's intuitive reasoning to which he can apply his single-stranded logic in order to identify the problem she has sensed. He can then count the cost of the probable solution, weigh this against the other factors he has already dealt with and come to a conclusion.

Then, generally speaking, both parties will be happy. They will not only be able to execute a decision from a broader basis of information, but they will have affirmed each other's worth. The wife will know that her opinion does count.

However, the sword cuts both ways. The wife who has presented her case and knows that her husband has seriously worked through all the data that she has presented, has an opportunity to affirm her husband's worth as a person and his role of leadership, even though she may be uncomfortable with his decision. And she can continue to do so even if the decision proves wrong. She can honestly state that he did the best he could with the facts at hand. There was evidently an issue that neither one of them could see. She may have 'felt it', but she is also aware that decisions cannot be based on feelings alone. The wife has a choice at this point: she can say, 'I told you so', in order to 'score points' in the hope of gaining more prestige in the decision-making process. Or she can affirm her husband's worth as a person.

The fact that men derive much of their self-worth from being respected for their competence and women gain a good deal of theirs from belonging, is a useful tool in meeting needs. It is one way of ensuring that we 'scratch where the other person is itching'. One might say that surely women derive some sense of self-worth through being respected for their competence—after all, aren't they proud of their needlework, their jams and preserves and the whiteness of their laundry? Aren't some women even 'house proud'? This is true, but we suspect that in most well-balanced marriages the husband takes more pride in his wife's accomplishments than she does (unless he is threatened by them). We suspect that the origin of the expertise of many a wife can be traced back to an initial desire to please her husband, and the failure of a husband to recognize his wife's attempts to please him is a great source of irritation and hurt. In fact, one of the most common instigating factors in unfaithfulness among wives, is the assumption that their husbands didn't appreciate them, so they would find someone who did.

The husband who walks in the front door and is greeted by a wife who states she spent the whole day cleaning out the glory-hole should (a) recognize that this is an act of love towards him, and (b) go and look at the glory-hole and show appreciation as an act of love towards her. Husbands who reckon their wives clean out the glory-hole because they cannot stand the mess are only partially right. What they fail to recognize is that it stems from their overall desire to be a 'worthy partner', just as the husband continually strives for pay rises because he sees a good provider as a worthy partner.

The art of 'scratching where someone else is itching' is not totally limited to understanding the difference between a male and a female mind set. People are different, as well. Expressions of love go far beyond demonstrating appreciation for accomplishments. Some people have a need for verbal expressions of love. They want to hear the words, 'I love you.' In the play, *Fiddler On The Roof*, Tevye says to his spouse, 'Do you love me?' And she replies something to the effect of, 'After all these years, to ask a question like that!' He presses the point and says, 'Do you *love* me?' and she replies that she has been washing his laundry and preparing his meals and taking care of his kids—and still he says, 'But do you love me?' Evidently, acts alone did not meet his needs.

For others, words in themselves do not meet their needs. Some feel loved because their partner is willing just to spend time with them. A husband may express his love by working long hours to provide for material needs, and yet his wife may say, 'Fine—we've got a big house and two cars. But you're never around when I need you.'

Loyalty in little things shows love. It used to be, when we were driving down the road, that I (Dave) would become irritated with another driver's antics and would say something like, 'You sorry bear-hugger!' Whereupon Joyce would immediately defend the other driver with statements like, 'Well, perhaps he couldn't see from that angle', or 'Maybe he's had a bad day.' Until one day I said, 'Who are you married to, me or the guy in the other car?' She got the message. The next time I 'cussed out' another driver, she immediately chimed in, 'Yeah, what a crazy chicken-plucker he is!' Naturally, the absurdity of it had us in fits of laughter, and has just about broken me of the habit; but at least she is not 'taking up' for other drivers!

On the other hand, Joyce really loves to be surprised with cut flowers. Potted ones are nice, but not quite as good as cut flowers. You see, Joyce, by her own admission, has a 'brown thumb' and could probably kill a giant redwood if it were dependent upon her for its nurture. She does well with cut flowers and has developed quite a flare for arrangements. She loves to have these flower arrangements around the house. For years I could see little wisdom in investing in flowers which were doomed to wilt in a comparatively short space of time. Consequently when I wanted to show her I loved her, I would bring her a box of candy. I thought chocolates were much nicer than daffodils, and after all, I could help her eat the chocolates. Over the years, two things have happened to help me change my mind. One is that I now have as much of a problem keeping my weight down as she does. The other, and much more important, is that I finally got smart. I realized that it was not flowers I was investing in, it was my wife. A pound or so spent periodically on seasonal cut flowers is a judicious investment in her happiness. It meets her needs. I may not understand it; I do not particularly want people getting me cut flowers; but then, that is a message of love that she understands.

I (Joyce) am so glad he finally got the message! I realize cut flowers do not speak to every woman, but they certainly do to me. However, there is one anomaly in a woman's needs which fortunately Dave understood right from the beginning of our relationship (at least, he understood what to *do*!). I suppose nothing frustrates a man more than the quick-changing moods of his wife. This is especially so when he asks 'What's wrong?' and her reply is, 'I don't know.' Troublesome as this is, a lot of the time it is true. You may feel you do not understand your wife—and you are probably right. But would it make you feel any better if she said, 'I don't understand myself either'? There are times when a woman feels like crying and honestly does not know why. The accompanying feelings may be insecurity, loneliness, depression, rejection—but with no logical foundation for these feelings. I have thought about this a lot, and the closest I can narrow it down is to something like feelings of insecurity and aloneness. Here is where a husband can really minister to his wife, and it is not necessary to understand her at all. It is really very simple: just come alongside your wife, put your arms around her and hold her close. You do not need to say anything—just hold her. There is something in the way that God made Eve for Adam that makes this simple gesture speak volumes. It says that he is her protector, her strength, her friend, her comfort; it reinforces in a woman just how much she needs her man. It makes her feel loved, protected and understood. I have found, in talking to women from all around the world, that this is not a cultural characteristic; it goes beyond culture and social customs. I do not understand it, but it is just the way we are. It is a very easy need to meet. I guess we just need to be drawn back into the ribs that we came from. We are different—aren't you glad?

For further consideration

Do we express love in ways that are understood by each other?

Does my way of expressing love meet your needs?

Chapter 15

One Flesh

It was God who invented sex, not the people who make a living out of it. The Church for the most part has been guilty of 'throwing out the baby with the bath-water'. This is because, in a lot of instances, instead of being men and women who act confidently on God's word, we have become reacters. When something is abused the natural tendency of many of us is to avoid it altogether so as not to be 'tarred with the same brush'. Happily, the Church is coming out of this long dark tunnel and there are Christian leaders who are willing to speak openly on this subject.

There is a fair amount of evidence that godly, honestly committed Christian scholars have a more well-rounded understanding of the heart and mind of God today than ever before in Church history. We cannot look to Victorian Christianity for help on this subject, nor to the Reformation, or even to the early Church Fathers; but we must go back to God and his word.

God instituted sex, his word instructs us in sex, it celebrates sex, and it limits sex. The problem came early in the Church when a healthy Judaeo-Christian concept of sex was tarnished by Greek philosophy, which evidently came along part-and-parcel with the vast numbers of new Greek converts. This Greek philosophy said basically that what is spiritual is good, what is physical is bad; all matter is sinful, the body is matter, and therefore the body is sinful. Consequently, anything to do with the body is sinful.

For instance, Augustine wished that God had planned the means of human reproduction which was 'less embarrassing' than sexual intercourse. (See Simone de Beauvoir, *The Second Sex*, Alfred A. Knopf Inc., p.156.) Augustine tried to imagine some other way that reproduction would have occurred, had the human race not fallen into sin—perhaps something like plant pollination. In his book *The City of God* Augustine describes in detail what he believes 'the act of generation' would have been like in paradise if Adam and Eve had not disobeyed God.... Christian leaders of the first few centuries after Christ actually taught that sex organs had been personally designed by the devil and that their 'horrible appearance' proved it! Others (Jerome, John Chrysostom and Gregory of Nyssa among them) taught that God's original plan had been for mankind to reproduce in an angelic fashion.... Jerome would not permit married couples to partake of the Eucharist for several days after performing the 'bestial act' of intercourse.... Jerome told husbands, 'if we abstain from coitus we honour our wives; if we do not abstain, well—what is the opposite of honour but insult?' (See Letha Scanzoni, *Sex and the Single Eye*, Zondervan, pp.27, 30 and 31.)

One of the ways to encourage celibacy among the early saints was to encourage an analytical focus on physical beauty. Chrysostom once wrote in a letter to a young man considering marriage:

> The ground work of this corporal beauty is nothing else but phlegm and blood and humour and bile, and the fluid of masticated food.... If you consider what is stored up inside those beautiful eyes, and that straight nose, and the mouth and cheeks, you will affirm that the well-shaped body is nothing else than a whitened sepulchre.... Moreover, when you see a rag with any of these things on it such as phlegm or spittle, you cannot bear to touch it even with the tips of your fingers, nay

176

you cannot endure looking at it; are you then in a flutter of excitement about the storehouses and repositories of these things? (Chrysostom, *Letters to Theodore*, quoted in Morton M. Hunt, *The Natural History of Love*, Alfred A. Knopf Inc., p.110.)

Naturally, to make these statements the early church fathers had to ignore completely passages such as Genesis 2:24 which states, 'The two shall become one flesh' (*before* the fall) or the next verse which tells us that 'they were naked and felt no shame'. It also ignores Psalm 139:14 where David praised God because he is fearfully and wonderfully made. The statements also failed to take into account Paul's fascination with the intricacy of the body in 1 Corinthians 12. Paul did recommend special modesty in verse 23 for less presentable parts of our body, but he certainly did not recommend disowning them. He did not have a low view of the body. On the contrary, in Romans 6:13 he states, 'Do not offer the parts of your body to sin, as instruments of wickedness, but rather offer yourselves to God, as those who have been brought from death to life; and offer the parts of your body to him as instruments of righteousness.' It would seem the very parts of our body that get us into trouble can be offered to God as instruments of righteousness.

The effects of Greek philosophy continued on long after the early church fathers. During the Middle ages the church was still in a long dark tunnel concerning the body itself and sex in particular.

Complete abstinence from sex relations had to be maintained on no less than five days out of the seven; on Thursdays in memory of the arrest of our Lord, on Fridays in commemoration of his death, on Saturdays in honour of the Blessed Virgin, on Sundays in honour of the resurrection, and on Mondays in honour of the faithful departed. (Ernest C. Messinger, 'The Mystery of Sex and Marriage in Catholic Theology', Vol. 2 in *Two in One Flesh*, Newman Press, p.152.)

At the same time, newly married couples were encouraged to abstain on the wedding night in honour of the Virgin Mary as well. Some said the Holy Spirit left the room when a couple engaged in intercourse even for the sole purpose of conceiving a child.

When I (Dave) read this to the young men in my Monday night Bible Study, they said, 'Who did you say those guys were that made those statements?'

'The early Church Fathers,' I said.

Their reply: 'I don't understand how they fathered anything with an attitude like that!'

Constant faithful study of the Scriptures has enabled us to separate God's principles and intentions from human traditions based on pagan philosophy. First, we need to ask ourselves, what was God's purpose for sex? We see four: procreation, reuniting, vulnerability and pleasure.

Procreation: In Genesis 1:28 God told Adam: 'Be fruitful and increase in number; fill the earth.' There are some questions about this very simple command which we are not absolutely sure we can answer. The first question is, does it mean immediately? Does a couple have to get started on a family within the first year? Or can they use contraceptives in order to be able to start the family at what may be a more opportune time? This question is very closely linked to the next, which is, is the earth filled? God said be fruitful and multiply *and fill the earth*. To many, the fact that we are constantly facing issues of over-population and diminishing resources is proof enough that this command has already been fulfilled.

These are questions that we cannot answer categorically. Indeed, it would take an entire book just to make a good attempt at it. However, there are some things to consider before we leap one way or the other, or encourage couples to do so.

The first deals with the contraceptive issue. If a couple does not believe in taking advantage of medical science for the healing of their bodies, then they should definitely not take advantage of medical science for birth control. It would be out of step with the rest of their beliefs. Another issue that has to be faced is the fact that even the 'rhythm method' is, in fact, birth control. It is taking advantage of medical science in that it recognizes that women ovulate approximately halfway between menstrual periods, and that therefore sexual intercourse should be avoided during a four or five day period. A further sophistication of this involves a woman taking her temperature every morning in order to plot a graph that indicates when she is ovulating. Still, it is a form of birth control; but when you think of it, just plain abstinence is a form of birth control when preventing conception is the reason for abstaining.

Of course, there are problems with the rhythm method, as illustrated by the old one-liner:

'What do you call people who use the rhythm method?' Answer: 'Parents.'

However, many people feel it is unspiritual to use any kind of device, chemical or pill, for contraception. There are certainly some considerations that need to be taken into account before using these more sophisticated devices. The first one only applies to Roman Catholics, and that is, how do you relate to your church authority?

It is only safe to take the Pill for five to seven years. Diaphragms and contraceptive foams are not a hundred per cent foolproof. Condoms reduce sensation for the male; however, this can be an advantage as it tends to delay ejaculation. Surgical procedures such as vasectomies and tying Fallopian tubes are not a hundred per cent reversible and therefore are generally limited to couples who feel they have finished having children.

There are also the intra-uterine devices, which, in actuality, keep the uterus open, which means egg and sperm can actually come together and be fertilized. However, pregnancy will not be successful because the uterus cannot close. This, in fact, brings about a very early abortion each time fertilization takes place. If you hold the scriptural view that life begins when egg and sperm come together, then you must regard these devices as definitely out of line for a Christian.

We are not very excited about the concept of people getting married and planning not to have children just out of pure selfishness so that they will not have to share their lives and resources with a larger family. We have already quoted Malachi 2:15, where God said he wants godly offspring. A couple who honestly believe they are not to have children in order to give themselves to the ministry, are not suffering from selfish motivation and should not be made to feel guilty over this.

Because procreation is the most obvious purpose for sex, some people think it is the only purpose.

Reuniting: Adam was made from the dust of the ground (Gen 2:7), but Eve was made from Adam's flesh and bone (Gen 2:22–25). Adam said, 'This is now bone of my bones and flesh of my flesh.' In other words, 'She is a part of me', and Adam was incomplete without her. Sexual relationships are the physical expression of the completeness that is experienced in marriage.

'God created man in his own image...male and female created he them' (Gen 1:27, AV). Not all the qualities of God that he was passing along to mankind were present in Adam. Therefore, Adam was incomplete. Marriage is a spiritual union, but on the feeling level sex is an expression of this reunion, both psychological and physical. It is the physical celebration of this reuniting.

This reuniting is a major manifestation of the fact that we were created as relational beings. Genesis 2:18 tells us, 'It is not good for the man to be alone.' Unrelated humanity was the first thing that God condemned. He took a rib out of the man, fashioned him a mate, and reunited them.

Vulnerability: 'The man and his wife were both naked, and they felt no shame' (Gen 2:25). This is not a plea for nudist colonies! Real vulnerability begins in the heart; Adam and Eve were innocent, they had not sinned against

180

God or each other—they had no hang-ups. It is very significant that after the Fall Adam and Eve had problems with nakedness—especially when you consider that they were the only two humans around. If I have a clear conscience before my partner, I have nothing to fear: I can be vulnerable. I believe that God desires vulnerability because he knows it requires a clear conscience. Vulnerability is a necessary ingredient in relationships. The greater the capacity for vulnerability, the greater the possibility for depth in a relationship.

Sex is certainly physical vulnerability. Physically, one cannot be more vulnerable. Fortunately, there is more to sex than physical vulnerability. It also takes vulnerability of the heart. The less vulnerability in our hearts, the more difficult is the physical vulnerability, and sex can become impossible.

It is not difficult, therefore, to see why sex problems are seldom ever sex problems, but relationship problems where vulnerability of the heart has been stifled. Counsellees who come with relationship problems almost never have good sex lives, and the reverse is true. People who come with sex problems are almost always found to have relationship problems.

Vulnerability, strangely enough, leads to security. When we leave the security of our parental homes, we become vulnerable; but this vulnerability is a commitment to our new partner. We are saying, 'I will make myself completely vulnerable and commit myself entirely to you.' Genesis 2:24 says: 'For this reason a man will leave his father and mother and be united to his wife, and they will become one flesh.' The commitment to vulnerability is sealed through a physical act of vulnerability.

This commitment is being challenged today by both the 'Playboy culture' and the Women's Lib. movement. The question is asked, 'Why should I make myself so vulnerable as to stake my future on the fortunes of another?' Both these groups have a very hedonistic outlook and view the opposite sex as something designed to meet their needs, to be used as long as it is convenient. For them, sex is no celebration of life and commitment, but is an escape from life. Sometimes it is prescribed as though it were a tranquillizer.

This concept is what some call 'recreational sex'. And God prohibits recreational sex in his commandments forbidding both adultery and fornication. This is not done by a God who is a 'kill-joy' and does not want people to have fun. It is done by a very loving heavenly Father with a view towards complete sexual fulfilment.

Ever since the beginning of time, men especially have been trained to advance themselves by taking advantage of chinks in their opponents' armour. No one removes his armour as long as there is competition. Today we live in a world that is more competitive than it has ever been. We seem to be in competition from dawn until dusk. In some families it begins by competing for the bathroom first thing in the morning. We compete in traffic on the way to work and for promotion at work, and then we come home and even choose forms of relaxation, such as bridge and golf, which involves competition. Vulnerability means taking off our armour.

Consequently, there has got to be one place where there is no competition, and that is in bed. These prohibitions against recreational sex were designed to ensure that we do not feel competition in bed. We can become completely vulnerable with our partner, because we know our performance, technique and anatomy are not being compared against another partner. At least that is the way God intended it. Those who have had a problem in this area must commit it to a very loving Father and ask that he remove the old memories from our mind and allow us complete vulnerability. We have seen this happen even with some of the most promiscuous people.

The wonderful thing about this vulnerability is that it allows us to affirm the worth of our partner in a very special way. Vulnerability and affirmation go hand in hand. We give our trust to those individuals whom we esteem to be of worth. For instance, it always makes me feel special if someone hands me the keys to his new car, because I feel like I am being singled out as a person who is trustworthy. A person who does this is affirming a special quality in me. How much more when a man and a woman make themselves completely vulnerable to one another in this very special way.

For many, Paul's words in Ephesians 5:31–32 really are a mystery: '"For this reason a man will leave his father and mother and will be united to his wife, and the two will become one flesh." This is a profound mystery—but I am talking about Christ and the Church.' Not only is Paul talking about marriage, but he picks the one passage from Genesis that seems to be speaking specifically about sex, and then says that he is talking about Christ and the Church. How does Christ's relationship with the Church correlate with the act of marriage? Paul says, 'For the message of the cross is foolishness to those who are perishing, but to us who are being saved it is the power of God' (1 Corinthians 1:18). It does no disservice to this passage to take some of the words out of it and come up with the statement, 'The message of the cross…is the power of God.' That is not out of context, but it, too, is a very mysterious statement. The God who spoke through rumbling mountains, parted the Red Sea, opened up the earth to swallow thirty thousand people—now demonstrates his power through dying? This is it: the Lord of glory came to earth and began by making himself vulnerable to a teenage Jewish maiden, depending on her to change his nappies, and wound up so vulnerable on the cross that he could not even wipe the sweat from his brow. And this is the power of God, this extreme vulnerability. God so loved me that he sent his Son to be completely vulnerable to all that men would do to him. It was through this vulnerability that he affirmed my worth as a person. This is the message of the New Testament: that the gospel is not communicated from a position of superiority, it is communicated from a position of vulnerability. And when Paul says, 'I speak of a mystery,' I believe this is the correlation: the most vulnerable thing he could do, being correlated with the most vulnerable thing we can do to affirm each other's worth as people. I also believe this is why Satan misses no opportunity to smear sex, to cheapen it, to remove this really deep vulnerable unity, and replace it with a cheap substitute in the form of recreational sex.

Pleasure: Pleasure, because of the fulfilment of our need to relate and the joy of complete vulnerability. Here is where the Christian reacters come in: 'The world enjoys sex—certainly we should not.' Or, 'We might enjoy it, but we should not indulge in it for that very reason.' Or, worse yet, 'It might be all right to enjoy it, but it's not something to admit to.' And on it goes, even down to, 'It might be all right, but certainly that wasn't part of God's intended purpose.'

Well, it certainly would appear that that *was* part of God's intended purpose. The Song of Solomon is not exactly the place where you would want your eight-year-olds to begin their Quiet Times! Explaining procreation to an eight-year-old is one thing; but for *this* aspect of sex, I would rather wait a year or two! This book of love clearly demonstrates the delight a married couple can have in each other's bodies. Some say this book was written solely as an allegory of Christ's relationship with the Church. Others says it is purely a comment on married love. Frankly, we think it is both. In fact, there are several areas in the Bible where the writers seem to go back and forth, because God makes such a strong parallel between a marriage and Christ's relationship with the Church.

However, it makes little difference what you believe. If the book is a commentary on married sex, then it teaches us that God intended this relationship for pleasure. If it is an allegory of Christ's relationship to the Church, then it still shows that God intended sex for pleasure. Would God correlate his love for the Church with a romantic sex life if a

184

romantic, pleasurable sex life was not normal in God's economy? That is illogical!

Let us look at a further bit of logic. If you do not believe that sex was intended for pleasure, or that at least it was a part of God's intended purpose, then you must remove it from all relationship aspects of a marriage and limit it only to procreation, because the other two aspects that we have named—vulnerability and reconciliation—both bring pleasure and are enhanced by pleasure. If pleasure is ruled out and sex is limited to procreation, you not only have a difficult time justifying the Song of Solomon, but you have an even harder time with Proverbs 5:18–19, which says, 'May your fountain be blessed, and may you rejoice in the wife of your youth. A loving doe, a graceful deer—may her breasts satisfy you always, may you ever be captivated by her love.' If sex is limited to procreation, then all the equipment on a woman's body which is dissimilar to a male, but complementary, is only for the purpose of pro-creation and nurture, and consequently one has to say that this scripture is by a middle-aged man (because he is no longer a youth) who is still breast-feeding!

One of the most fascinating testimonies I have ever heard was that of a woman who was 'frightfully British' who began her testimony by saying, 'I won't tell you how old I am; but I'd like to tell you what the baptism in the Holy Spirit will do for your sex life.' (Subsequently she told us that she was seventy-seven years old.) She said, 'Ten years ago'—when she was a spring chicken of sixty-seven—'I realized that the fact that I didn't really enjoy sex took a lot of enjoyment out of it for my husband, as well.' Of course, he was a lot younger than she was—five years. 'So I asked the Lord to make sex an enjoyable thing for me.' And then she said, 'He certainly answered that prayer. It's been getting better and better all the time.' And then she looked around with her eyes twinkling and said, 'In fact, last night was the best!' She had not been willing to tell her age—but she had been willing to talk about the quality of the previous night's sex. Now *that's* a liberated woman!

I like that testimony for several reasons. One is that it blows the myth that sex is something that ends at middle-age. It also attests to the fact that God answers prayer regarding the pleasurable aspect of sex. It shows that God is interested in every aspect of our lives.

Reconciliation: 'It is better to marry than to burn' (1 Cor 7:9). Sometimes we suspect that our physical need to relate is a strong enough motivation to overcome wounded pride and, in the words of an American Indian, 'bury the hatchet'. This physical side of our need to relate is a strong magnet pulling us towards reconciliation.

This is why masturbation is not good, even in marriage, because it allows marriage partners to become independent of each other; and we have even had this come up in counselling sessions.

Problem areas

I (Joyce) would like to look at a few things that might cause us to be lacking pleasure in our sex life.

Physical: Sometimes we are genuinely tired. The children keep us running from dawn till dusk, and then a good deal of the night. Sometimes this can be remedied simply by taking a nap when the children take a nap. Sometimes a physical check-up might be in order. Many women are borderline anaemics and would do well just to take iron tablets and possibly some multiple vitamins. At other times we can be put off because of poor hygiene; bad breath or body odour do not enhance romance. Simply brushing our teeth and having a wash before going to bed can do wonders for our love life! This, incidentally, is an area where we can practise the art of gentle confrontation. There is nothing traumatic about saying, 'Honey, I have a problem I think you can help me with. Would you mind brushing your teeth before we make love?'

Intellectual: Not having God's view of sex can put the

186

whole situation into a wrong perspective for us. Wrong thinking in this area needs to be dealt with, just as it does with self-esteem. We need to get a firm grasp on the facts and ask God to help us deal with faulty concepts.

Spiritual: We can simply be out of fellowship. I know that the closer I am to the Lord, the more pleasure I have in sex. This is because there certainly is a spiritual dimension to the act of marriage, and simply being out of fellowship tends to drag it down to a lower plane.

Emotional: Sometimes I have bad feelings about myself. If I do not love me, I do not think that Dave should, either. And bad feelings about our partner can be the greatest cause of resentment.

It begins like this: something happens at breakfast, maybe the toast is burnt or he says something that does not go down quite right, and there are words—angry words. He jerks on his coat, grabs his briefcase, walks out of the door and slams it; and she stands there with one clenched fist on each hip, glaring after him. He lurches out of the drive, goes down the block, through a roundabout and into the traffic. His mind begins to get enmeshed in the business of getting to work and dealing with the traffic, and by the time he reaches the office, he has completely forgotten about the argument.

But she has not forgotten about it. She is steaming. And she scrapes the breakfast dishes clean as if they are paper plates ready to be disposed. She pushes them into the washing-up water and scrubs at them furiously, going over in her mind what she said, and what he said, and what she should have said, and what she is going to say when he gets home and how he is going to respond to that, and then what she is going to say in return. She rehearses the conversation and all the possible alternative conversations; it is as though she is mapping out a game of chess—'If he moves this piece, then I'll do this'—or she is a general planning a battle, working out just where to place all the heavy artillery. And all day long, as she vacuums the house and picks up the clothes, she is placing cannons here and there. By the time late afternoon comes around, she has worked out the perfect strategy; and if nothing else, she is going to be cool…calm and collected. She is going to present herself completely unruffled.

So she gets dinner ready, gets dressed, and just *waits*.

And here he comes. He walks in the door, drops his briefcase. He has a smile on his face as if to say, 'Here I am, you lucky little woman!' *He has forgotten all about it.* But she has not forgotten. And she is cool, very cool. Pretty soon he begins to notice, and he says, 'What's the matter?' You know the answer she gives…'Nothing….' But he gets the message. He gets cold dinner and cold shoulder.

Then he flops in front of the television set with his cup of coffee. The evening passes. He keeps scratching his head and trying to remember. And then he says, 'Oh, yeah! Yeah, there was something said this morning, wasn't there…?'

By this time, it is bedtime, and he wants to make up. And you know how he does it? Out goes his arm, and he reaches around and wants a cuddle. This is his way of saying, 'I'm sorry.' But that is not her way. God made us different. Reconciliation, for a man, is sometimes through the act of marriage; but women have to have it verbalized. The man's approach is good: there is a magnetism to pull us together; but there is also the need to put the relationship right with words.

But by this time, her 'cool' is wearing off; so she acquiesces. They make love. But she is not happy about it. In fact, somehow she feels cheated. But hubby is satisfied; he thinks everything is reconciled. But she does not. And the next evening, they make love again; and she is still not satisfied. The next thing you know, sex begins to be a problem for her, which in turn creates a problem for him. But they have not got a sex problem at all: they have a relationship problem. To put things right, there is a need to verbalize, otherwise resentment gets a foothold. This is the reason for the admonition in Ephesians not to let the sun go down on your wrath; don't give the devil a foothold. And this is the way he gets a foothold in the bedroom.

Satanic: It has been quite a few years since I shared this at a women's meeting, and when I did, I found many women had had, or were experiencing, the same problem. I feel it needs to be shared any time it is appropriate. This country is riddled with Satanists and all manner of occult groups who are praying for the breakdown of Christian marriages.

About twelve years ago I went into a spell where not only did I not enjoy sex, I just did not want anything to do with it. There was nothing wrong with our relationship, I loved David as much as I ever had, but I had got to the point where I did not even want him to put his arm around me for fear it would lead to something further. I made every excuse in the book. I would go to bed early, go to bed late, have a headache or an upset stomach, and if I did finally feel it was necessary to make love, I would just sort of grit my teeth and get through it. One night we began and I just broke down in tears. I had to tell Dave that there was something drastically wrong, and I did not know what it was; that it was not that I did not love him, but I just had a real problem. Fortunately, he was very understanding. He said, 'Well, that's all right. Let's forget it tonight. Just go to sleep, and we'll talk about it tomorrow.'

The next evening, we discussed it. Fortunately, we were in a church that had had some good teaching on spiritual warfare. David knew what to do. He prayed over me; he took authority over Satan and we prayed together, and I have never seen anything so dramatic in my life. We went to bed—and we had a great time. It had been a real spiritual battle. Satan had been trying to rob us of what God had provided; but he was not able to, because of the power of prayer.

When John and June came on a Weekend they heard this part of the talk and realized that it related to them. June was totally uninterested in sex yet they knew it was not because of anything wrong in their relationship. But when we got their survey back, they claimed a 33% improvement in their marriage because, to put it in their words, they had 'kicked Satan out of the bedroom window'.*

Sexual problems are usually relationship problems, but occasionally they are genuinely physical in nature. We must emphasize that these problems belong to both the marriage partners. Situations like impotency, vaginal spasms or yeast infections should never be considered the sole responsibility of the one 'maintaining the equipment'.

Although the problems just named are physical in nature, they are frequently psychological in origin and can certainly be compounded by a partner who tends to blame rather than be understanding and supportive. Bob and Sherry, the couple we mentioned in the chapter on forgiveness (chapter 11), also had a sexual problem. As we said, he was undisciplined and insensitive, and she was bitter about it. By nature she was rather nervous, and this added to her tension.

Their problems were compounded in that over the previous three years she had suffered almost perpetual yeast infections. Every time one would clear up, it seemed that intercourse would cause it to flare back up again. The gynaecologist had given her every remedy known to mankind without success. There seemed to be no relief in sight. However, it seemed that the more they learned to demonstrate love and respect for one another, the less they were plagued with the yeast infection.

Our theory is that because Sherry had a very nervous

* Our initial information regarding Satanists praying for the breakdown of Christian marriages came several years ago when we received word that a large Satanists' 'prayer meeting' was to be convened. We attempted to verify this information and our search led us back to a pastor in London who stated that a recent convert in his congregation had been involved with Satanist activities and had been invited to this Halloween meeting. We were convinced at the time that this was not mere heresay and subsequent discussions with Christian leaders have led us to believe that this type of activity still continues.

190

temperament the tension in her marriage created tension in her body which actually changed the acid alkaline balance. This imbalance then made her vulnerable to the yeast infection. Consequently in a marriage where a wife suffers in this way, a husband who does nothing but complain and blame his wife for her inability to participate sexually is actually 'cutting off his own nose'. The same is true with impotency. A man may temporarily become impotent due to job pressure, tiredness, alcohol, etc, but a blaming, shaming attitude will put him under so much pressure to 'perform' that he will not be able to do so. Problems must be shared by a supportive, encouraging partner.

Care and maintenance of a sex life

Pleasurable sex is something that God intended but pleasurable sex is an achievement. It is the result of a process of constantly determining and communicating our needs. For most people, sex in early marriage presents no problem (with the exception of possible wedding night complications). From a sexual aspect, the honeymoon may last two or three years. When the newness wears off, we settle into a routine. This routine is generally based on a superficial observation of each other's needs and a low expectation of sexual fulfilment. It creates a very blinkered view of sex and takes no account of the fact that both partners are changing and, hopefully, growing. This could better be described as a rut rather than just a routine.

When we were first married, a doctor told us that if we were to keep a jar by the bed and place a bean in the jar every time we made love together in the first year, and then remove one bean from the jar every time we made love in subsequent years, we would never live long enough to get all the beans out of the jar. Well, we are happy to report that with us, at least, that is purely a fable. However, it is a fable which is based on the fact that people do get their sex lives in a rut, because of a lack of understanding, and we are aware that this same lack of understanding has caused some people's sex life to be a failure from the very beginning. Let us consider three specific areas of misunderstanding: outlook, aura and enactment.

The outlook of sex

Our outlook on sex is very important; it is part of a complete Christian world view. The Bible should influence every part of our life and certainly something that is so important to the vitality of our marriage. Paul says, 'The husband should fulfil his marital duty to his wife, and likewise the wife to her husband. The wife's body does not belong to her alone but also to her husband. In the same way, the husband's body does not belong to him alone but also to his wife' (1 Cor 7:3–4). This passage is obviously considering sex in the context of pleasure, but it does more than that, it gives a very good foundation for a Christian outlook on sex. The context of this passage implies that the husband and wife are actually indebted to each other, to meet each other's sexual needs. The responsibility for taking care of sexual need is not directed at the one with the need, but at the one whose responsibility it is to fulfil it. This is diametrically opposed to John's statement about the world's mentality: 'For all that is in the world, the lust of the flesh, and the lust of the eyes, and the pride of life, is not of the Father, but is of the world' (1 Jn 2:16, AV). John speaks about the fleshly focus and selfish desires of the carnal mind. Compare this with the complete shift in attitude in a Christian marriage where husbands and wives perceive sex not as a right, but as a responsibility. In other words, society says, 'I have sexual desires and expectations, and I have a right to have these fulfilled. My concern with the individual fulfilling these needs is limited to what is profitable in assuring that my needs are met.' The Christian outlook, on the other hand, is, 'I have a responsibility to meet my partner's needs.'

This shift in focus alone puts sex in its rightful place. It removes sex from the animal world and brings it into a world of romance and real love. This basic Christian concept serves as a platform from which to make further decisions regarding our sex life. For instance, questions of what should and should not be done regarding certain sexual practices, *where the Bible is silent,* must first of all be judged under the criterion of meeting the needs, desires and expectations of both partners. A certain practice which is desirable to one, may be either repugnant or painful to the other. If we apply the Christian rule of responsibility, the one who does not enjoy it must go ahead with it in order to meet the other partner's needs. However, the 'safety device' rests in the fact that the one with the desire also has a responsibility to meet their partner's needs and expectations. In other words, if each partner is putting the other first, the situation would never exist where one simply endures for the sake of the other.

This philosophy might sometimes seem to break down, especially where low expectations are concerned. For instance, if one partner has no desire to make love more than once every two months, while the other considers two to three times a week more suitable, it would seem that the option would fall to the one with the lowest expectation. However, this would be an abuse of the concept. The partner with the low expectation has a responsibility to pray that God will begin to change his or her desire. Simply to force low expectations on to our partner is exactly the same as forcing a high desire and unusual expectations on to our partner.

The fact that our partner has a responsibility to meet our needs, does not free us from the responsibility of communicating our needs. For instance, how can a husband become a giver in a sexual relationship if the wife does not admit to having any sexual needs or expectations?

There is a great tendency on the husband's part to place more emphasis on sex than love. Conversely, the woman tends to place more emphasis on what she considers to be love. We personally feel that if we could tie these two words tightly back together again, it would resolve the problem we have already discussed of low expectations. To a woman, the relationship is all important: it fulfils her need for belonging, and therefore anything that detracts from that is counterproductive. Sex must be seen to be the product of the relationship and not the purpose of it, otherwise women tend to feel used. They are not participants in a relationship but sex objects. Ann Landers, a very popular personal advice columnist in America, asked women to respond to a question, 'Would you be content to be held close and treated tenderly, and forget about "the act"? Answer yes or no.' 90,000 American women responded to this survey, and 72% of them said yes, they would be content to be held and cuddled. That is not saying that that number of women are uninterested in sex, it is saying that being held and cuddled is more important than intercourse itself. It does not say that the other 28% were not interested in being held close and being treated tenderly.

This brings us to what we will call the 'Doug Barnett gas ring' principle. Not that Doug is the first one to observe the principle, but as near as we know, he was the first to describe it in such elucidating terms. Women, claims Doug, are like a ring on an electric hob. You turn it on and it takes a while before it really gets up to full temperature. And after you turn it off, you can burn your hand on it five minutes later. Men, on the other hand, are like a gas ring, turn it on and vooom. And then when you turn it off, that is it, it cools right down. It takes women longer to get involved and they stay cuddly and snuggly for a long time afterwards. Men, on the other hand, seem to function as if they were in a high state of alert and ready to go at a moment's notice, and equally ready to roll over and go to sleep when the act is finished.

I bring this phenomenon up under the heading of outlook, because we are talking about meeting needs. This illustration probably represents the greatest unmet need. Proverbs 30:21–23 speaks about three things which cause the earth to tremble, and one of them is 'an unloved woman who is married'. This simply calls into focus the fact that if we are to maintain a Christian outlook and fix our attention on being sensitive givers, we must communicate needs and respond to needs.

It is not wrong to develop certain ideals and realistic expectations regarding our sex life, but it is wrong to develop unrealistic expectations. This is one of the greatest problems with pornography: it fosters unrealistic expectations, not just about what ought to occur in the bedroom, but about our partner. Let's face it, the woman in the centrefold of a men's magazine is frequently not quite as attractive as she is portrayed. After all, she is posed at her most flattering angle, in exactly the right lighting and little blemishes are removed when the photograph is developed. Even she cannot live up to those expectations. When we talk about pornography, we frequently see women with a smug look on their faces because they recognize that the type of pornography we have just discussed is very nearly limited to males, because males are more visually stimulated. However, rest assured that there is female pornography, and unfortunately it is much more socially accepted. Romance magazines are the female counterpart; they also develop unrealistic expectations that cannot be met in real life.

The aura of sex

The aura of sex includes an *aura of anticipation*. Clues given out in the morning are nice as they resurface during the day, making you look forward to the evening. The husband might make a comment such as, 'I hope we are not having anyone in tonight.' Or, 'See if you can keep the children from taking their nap today so they will go to sleep early tonight.' Or the wife might say, 'Don't be late tonight, dear.

I have planned a very special dinner for just the two of us.' Or either one of them might use a more straightforward approach, something like, 'Let's make an appointment for tonight.'

This brings up the question of the extent to which the wife should take the initiative. Quite frankly, most husbands are delighted at the thought of their wives 'seducing them'. After all, husbands like to feel that the act is not being carried out simply for their own pleasure. It is also good for a husband to know that he is still a highly desirable hunk of masculine protoplasm, and that his wife looks forward to making love with him. If the husband is the only initiator, then he begins to wonder just exactly how welcome his advances are. But the fact that the wife at least occasionally instigates sexual activity, goes a long way to removing this doubt from his mind.

The *aura of romance* adds the spice of adventure. A husband who comes home at night and is greeted at the door by a wife who is dressed very provocatively, smelling of their favourite perfume, imagines there is something up. Then when he sees a candlelit table, thoughtfully laid out for two, the best china and silver, his suspicions are confirmed. He is being 'seduced'. Isn't it great! It is a very creative and imaginative wife who is willing to do something adventuresome to keep their love life from getting into a rut. Proverbs 7:16–20 describes an adulteress enticing her lover with the following encouragements: 'I have covered my bed with coloured linens from Egypt. I have perfumed my bed with myrrh, aloes and cinnamon. Come, let's drink deep of love till morning; let's enjoy ourselves with love! My husband is not at home; he has gone on a long journey. He took his purse filled with money and will not be home till full moon.'

You wonder if this woman was this creative with her husband before her interest in her marriage dwindled. If she had been, he probably would not be going off on month long trips, and if he were absolutely forced to do so, he would take her along as well. The use of alluring decorations and spices was not limited to illicit encounters. The Song of Solomon speaks of these same exotic fragrances and practices—feeding each other spiced wine, walking out in the vineyards among the pomegranates, spending the night in the villages. All these things make married love very special and create variety. One worldly excuse for unfaithfulness is the statement, 'Variety is the spice of life.' The fact is, this variety can be introduced without changing partners.

Some of the things mentioned in the Song of Solomon may not sound very attractive to the western mind, but then I would not tell Joyce that her nose was like the Tower of Lebanon either. However, we have practised 'spending the night in the villages' (Song of Solomon 7:11)—we have simply gone to a small hotel for a romantic weekend. However, most of the time that is cost prohibitive. On the other hand, there is nothing that says you have to make love in the bedroom all of the time, there are other rooms in the house. The obvious caution here is security. Even if you feel you must stay in the bedroom, you can always experiment with the lighting.

The principle underlying the cultural clothing of the Old Testament is that you need to do things that make lovemaking very special. We do not need to spice it with cinnamon and aloes and myrrh, but we must spice it with variety.

The enactment of sex

Sexual intercourse is communication. It is the communication of love and respect. Most of us find it pretty difficult to sit down eyeball-to-eyeball and discuss in detail what we think ought to be going on in bed at night. Sexual intercourse itself gives a wonderful opportunity for communicating on the subject of sexual intercourse.

If my partner's body is not hers alone, but mine as well, as Paul says, then I have some right to move the parts around to the more desired position and so communicate my desires. She, of course, then has the right to send back counter-signals, such as, 'My arm will not bend that way.' A lot of embarrassment can be saved by paying heed to little tugs on the elbow or the knee, when we sense that our partner is physically requesting something that they cannot verbalize. A proper negative response is not just jerking away, but simply saying, 'I am not ready for that yet; wait a few minutes.' It may even be, 'Wait six months.' On the other hand, when something is pleasurable, a good response is, 'I'll give you half an hour to stop that.'

Husbands seem to be initiators most of the time, but wives can, and should, initiate, too. I am not speaking about initiating whether or not we have sex at all, but initiating moves designed to arouse our partner. However, it is difficult to say exactly what these moves designed to arouse should be. Men are all different, and what may arouse one may be like a bucket of cold water to another. However, there is one generalization that seems to have some validity, and that is that women seem to be sensitive all over their bodies, while men tend to be sensitive only in the genital area. However, this can be a source of 'disinformation', because a husband, in an attempt to arouse his wife, tends to concentrate on her genital area, while a wife, in an attempt to arouse her husband, may be running her hand up and down his back because that is what *she* likes.

There is no such thing as headship in sex relationships. Submission is mutual. Both must be sensitive to their partner and totally involved. Men do not want wives that they make love *to*, but wives that they make love *with*.

The important thing is communication; needs, expectations and desires cannot be met if they are not communicated. You could get a book like *The Act of Marriage* (Marshall Pickering) and read it together, and be especially observant of each other's reaction to different things. In the long run, sensitive communication pays off. Once we realize that when we are making love, we are actually communicating, then we become our own best teachers.

For further consideration

Faithfulness begins in our thought life. A conscious decision to allow ourselves to think romantically only about our partners will head off unfaithful actions.

What could we do to improve our sex life?

Chapter 16

Epilogue: About Marriage Weekends

Now that you have read the book is there any need to go on a Marriage Weekend? That would seem to be a logical question at this point. If we gave you our answer, that would just be our opinion. So let us examine some of the facts. First, if you are like most couples, you did not read this book together, as we suggested in the introduction. Second, there is also a good chance that you did not discuss the items at the end of each chapter. Third, there is a high probability that, if you did, the discussion was punctuated by the telephone, the children, or the nine o'clock news.

We give out 'critique' sheets at the end of our Marriage Weekends, where we ask nine general-information questions. These have been invaluable in helping us to shape the weekends to meet the greatest needs. The first question is, 'What part of the Weekend was most helpful?' We are always excited to think that someone has gained a new insight from one particular talk or another, and consequently we are anticipating answers like, the self-image talk, or the Christian view of sex, or the finance lecture, etc. However, one rather deflating answer comes back over and over again: 'Time spent alone with my partner.' This is something that is difficult to provide in book form, but Marriage Weekends do, by and large, give couples time alone to communicate.

Just how profitable are marriage weekends in general? We suppose that everyone who has conducted marriage weekends for any period of time has a large stack of glowing testimonies from people who have written back to say how helpful the weekends were. We have no doubt that all of us who conduct these weekends can point to couples who have quite dramatic changes in their relationships as a direct result of being on a weekend. Unfortunately, there is also the other end of the scale. Anyone who has done very many marriage weekends has sadly to report that at least one or two couples who have attended their weekends have eventually divorced; but one or two couples out of, say, five hundred, is a fairly complimentary statistic. On the other hand, being realistic, one must point out that generally people who attend marriage weekends are the least likely to become separated, for the simple reason that these are couples who recognize that a good marriage involves work and can never be taken for granted. We do have a large stack of glowing reports, and we are aware of one or two failures; but what about those couples in between—how profitable was their marriage weekend?

In order to gain data for this book we sent out a survey to 300 couples with whom we are still in contact, and received back 111 replies. The first question on this survey asked them to rate their marriage on a scale of one to ten prior to the Marriage Weekend, and then to give a current rating. We recognize that this is not the most scientific way to do things, because it is purely subjective, representing the couple's own opinion. However, the average improvement claimed by the couples answering the survey was 36·13%, which is a pretty significant rise.

We think this speaks volumes for the value of spending a weekend alone together as a couple in an environment conducive to communication, with a special emphasis on this very special relationship. Approximately 65% of the couples claim that the Marriage Weekend actually improved their relationship with God. This statistic on its own might surprise some, but because you have read the book, you understand that our relationship with God affects the way we live and conversely, our ability to change the way we live demands that we strengthen our relationship with God.

To us, the statistic which does the most to prove the superiority of a marriage weekend over simply reading a book, is the fact that well over 80% of those surveyed claimed to have a continued improved ability to communicate more effectively. It is also significant that the vast majority of those who claimed they did not have any improvement in their communication were couples who initially rated their marriage rather high, which would imply that they had less room for improvement.

Marriage weekends definitely produce results. Any couple interested in investing in their marriage relationship would certainly profit by one of these. In fact, some Christian leaders feel that couples should go on a marriage weekend at least once a year. Lee Carlson, who heads up the executive ministry for Campus Crusade for Christ in Great Britain, feels very strongly about this, so much so that, along with his wife Jan, they have developed 'in house' marriage weekends for couples involved in that ministry. However, they also encourage these couples to attend other weekends as well.

By this time, you may be 'sold' on the idea of going on a marriage weekend, and naturally we would like to see you on one of the Mission to Marriage Weekends conducted by Lighted Laymen, which pretty well follow the format of this book. However, although we personally enjoy hearing authors go over the same material in person that we have already read in their books, others may not. You may well decide you have heard all that Dave and Joyce Ames have to say, and you may like to hear what someone else is presenting. There are nine other organizations conducting marriage weekends in this country at this time. They vary in several aspects, much more so than we originally thought before we began to research the material for this chapter. The following paragraphs are an attempt to give you a thumbnail sketch of each weekend, in order to enable you to find the weekend you feel would suit you best. Appendix A gives you a complete list of contact points for further information.

Marriage Encounter: Three of the groups running marriage weekends in this country come under the heading of 'Marriage Encounter'; World Wide Marriage Encounter is the official name of the Catholic expression. There are also Anglican and Baptist expressions of Marriage Encounter.

Marriage Encounter is definitely the grandparent of all marriage weekends. Anyone who does a marriage weekend owes something to Marriage Encounter—if nothing else, at least the idea of having a marriage weekend.

Marriage Encounter was begun by a Roman Catholic priest in Spain in the early sixties, and it spread to South America, then up to North America. From there, it spread to many other countries and denominations which demonstrates its wide appeal. In January 1977, Joyce and I attended a Roman Catholic Marriage Encounter (the only one available at the time), with no intention whatsoever of being involved in this type of ministry. We recommended it to several other couples because we felt there was tremendous potential in husbands and wives listening to a presentation on a particular aspect of marriage and then having an opportunity to communicate on it at length in the privacy of their own rooms. In June of that year, we shared our feelings about Marriage Encounter with Jack Boggs, the pastor of a small American Southern Baptist church in our area. He and his wife Jo thought it would be a good idea to do a similar weekend for people in their church and the local American base chapel. So we teamed up with Jack and Jo Boggs in September 1977 at Hengrave Hall, in Suffolk, to use the Marriage Encounter format with teaching material similar to the contents of this book. We have heard similar stories from other people doing marriage weekends after having been involved in a Marriage Encounter. Most seemed to use the format and develop material to suit their own vision.

All Marriage Encounter weekends use a similar format, which consists of a series of presentations by team couples followed by a time of sharing between couples in the privacy of their own rooms. These presentations are given by the team couples who recount their own experiences of working through various aspects of marriage. Each presentation is built around a framework of well-recognized relationship principles which allow the introduction of as much biblical content as the presenting team desires. As team members share their thoughts, partners find the necessary encouragement to communicate with each other.

In the early days of Marriage Encounter in the USA, the driving force came from the prolific writings of Jesuit priest Chuck Gallager. Today, however, the popular author who probably best represents the thinking behind the material presented in Marriage Encounter weekends is the Jesuit priest and psychologist John Powell. Although the structure is similar, there is a definite variation between Catholic, Anglican and Baptist Marriage Encounter weekends. Catholic Marriage Encounters usually have three team couples plus a priest, and the priest shares his experience as one married to the Church. Anglican and Baptist Marriage Encounters generally have three or four team couples, but one of them is a clergy couple. Both Anglican and Catholic Marriage Encounters tend to represent Christianity more on the 'sacramental' side. The people on Anglican Marriage Encounters claim that they are beginning to see their weekends more and more as 'outreach'. Because they have not made a particularly heavy emphasis on the Christian content, more and more unchurched people have felt free to come on the weekends and have been subtly confronted by the claims of Christ.

The Baptists, on the other hand, claim that their expression of Marriage Encounter is one hundred per cent staffed by evangelical Christians and that the Bible is used as much as possible. However, they still hold to the general principle that the weekends are available for any couples who desire to improve their marriages.

All three expressions of Marriage Encounter conduct enough weekends a year to handle as many people as are interested. Marriage Encounter claims this is forty-four hours that will change your life, and we certainly know many, many couples who can attest to that truth.

Marriage Review: Richard and Joyce Conner, a lovely pair of young-at-heart senior citizens, regularly conduct marriage weekends called 'Marriage Review'. They also owe their inspiration to Catholic Marriage Encounter. Their weekends tend to be a bit smaller than the twenty or so couples who normally attend a Marriage Encounter. Their teaching is very Bible-based, and there is a refreshing atmosphere of informality about the entire weekend.

Anyone who conducts marriage weekends would probably claim that there is a certain amount of variation from weekend to weekend for the simple reason that people are not alike, and their needs vary. Even in a lecture situation speakers can sense differences in the needs of groups. However, Richard and Joyce Conner maintain a greater flexibility from weekend to weekend than Marriage Encounter or our own Christian Marriage Weekends. For instance, though for the most part they keep to the Marriage Encounter format, they will occasionally have small group discussions. Richard and Joyce have several other couples working with them, and they conduct Marriage Review weekends at various venues across the country throughout the year, with sufficient frequency to handle all those interested. Their weekends favour the charismatic frame of reference, and their profitability can be attested to by hundreds of couples who have attended.

Marriage Fulfilment: David and Joyce Huggett also organize retreats for married couples and at present are majoring on mid-week Marriage Fulfilment Retreats for clergy couples. For many clergy couples it is genuinely difficult to escape from the parish at weekends, so these retreats take place from early afternoon on Tuesday to after lunch on Thursday. The retreats have three basic ingredients: biblical teaching on marriage, plenty of opportunity for couples to be together to re-evaluate their relationship, and prayer ministry for any who wish to avail themselves of it. Time for relaxation is also built into the programme and opportunities are given for couples to assess how parish pressures are impinging on their marital relationship and what they can do practically to alleviate any strain and stress.

The value of such retreats is two-fold. First, they give support to clergy couples themselves. Secondly, as clergy couples find their love for one another deepening through such occasions, they encourage members of their congregation in the belief that working at the marriage relationship in such a context reaps rich dividends.

David and Joyce occasionally conduct Marriage Fulfilment weekends in local churches and are also heavily involved in marriage preparation, running Engaged Couples' Weekends in their own church. Joyce is a prolific writer in the field of marriage, and anyone reading her books will have little doubt about the soundness of their teaching. They have conducted workshops at major Christian conference centres and would be well worth inviting into a church that realizes the priority of marriage.

We are glad that they provide such a service. The whole concept of Christian marriage weekends seems to have a remedial stigma about it which none of us who conduct marriage weekends seems to be able to shake. Hopefully, clergy couples attending such a weekend will be able to disabuse their congregations of such nonsense. It has been our experience that the best possible way for a pastor to encourage his parishioners to attend a Christian marriage weekend is for him and his wife to attend one first. The logic is that if the pastor and his wife felt it worthwhile (who are presumed to be mature Christians with a good marriage) then it would be profitable for the rest of the congregation.

Lighted Laymen, Marriage Review and Care and Counsel also send teams to conduct weekends in local churches. This is an excellent means of exposing congregations to marriage teaching and frequently motivates a number of couples to attend a residential weekend. There are positive and negative aspects to this concept.

Positively: they reach people who would not be able to attend a residential weekend because of feeding babies, finances, or other considerations, and they are less expensive to conduct. They do take a bit of committee work on the part of the local church, but since there is no cost for a conference centre or long-term baby-minding, it is a relatively small expense compared to the cost of sending an equal number of couples off for a weekend. Also, they can be tailor-made for the requirements of the host church.

Negatively: it is impossible to provide the same carefree atmosphere of no phone, no children, no television and no responsibility, which is a much more conducive environment for effective communication. Nonetheless, these marriage weekends should not be dismissed lightly, because they do cause couples to consider the priority of their relationship, communication, and the fact that God is committed to their marriage.

The Association for Marriage Enrichment: this was formed in 1979 after David Mace (who founded Marriage Guidance) and his wife Vera had visited this country and trained a few couples in their method of running weekend retreats. These couples, together with some Anglicans who had also worked in this field, were the founders of the Association.

It is a direct descendant of the Association of Couples for Marriage Enrichment (ACME) which was formed in America in 1973 by the Maces. ACME worked with Quaker groups and others in the United Methodist Church who saw the need to promote the idea of growth in marriage and ensure the proper training of leader couples in as wide a context as possible.

In this country, AME has grown slowly from its small beginnings and now offers training in couple-leadership, retreats for five to eight couples at a time, and shorter introductory events.

Team members are, for the most part, committed Christians who conduct marriage weekends within a basically secular framework in order to reach couples of any or no religious persuasion. Here, couples have opportunities to reflect on their relationship and gain deeper understanding of themselves and their partners. AME believe that most marriages can be improved, and that the ability to respond to changing expectations in marriage requires new skills and insights.

Different counselling organizations, churches, etc, sponsor AME retreats, and generally these are open to all couples committed to their own relationship. The approach is non-judgemental and designed to enable couples to continue to grow together, both as individuals and as a couple, in all aspects of their relationship, including the spiritual and moral.

Care and Counsel: this organization presently has a number of couples who have been prepared by the Association for Marriage Enrichment, who conduct marriage weekends with a definite Christian stance. They are trained to be sensitive to each individual as a whole person: a thinking, feeling and spiritual being. They are all committed Christians who try to relate their Christian faith to their experiences and to help others to do so as well. One of the couples, Roy and Jan Stafford, has attended one of our weekends and was therefore able to provide some comparisons. The first and most obvious difference is that Care and Counsel, as a matter of policy, conduct their weekends with rather small groups, usually five couples and a presenting couple. They claim that not only is this more informal, but it also provides the potential to work in greater depth. The

Staffords stated that the Christian content is less overt on their weekends than on our particular presentation. This may be a plus factor for some couples, especially where one partner is less disposed towards Christian teaching.

Roy and Jan Stafford: this couple have developed a specialized ministry because of their missionary background and Jan's membership of the staff of All Nations Bible College. While serving with the Care and Counsel weekend programme, they have acquired a particular interest in marriage enrichment for those preparing for, or engaged in, 'full-time' Christian ministry in Britain and overseas. They run seminars for theological students, for those training for cross-cultural missions (both long-term and short-term volunteers), and for those in missionary refresher courses. One of these seminars took place in Kenya for serving missionaries, others have been run for missionaries on leave. Their hope and prayer is that the marriages and ministry of those facing the joys and difficulties of cross-cultural life and work will be enriched.

Married Couples Weekends: Don and Heather Double of Good News Crusade conduct what is possibly the most atypical marriage weekend, which they call 'Married Couples Weekends'. For a start, the weekends are considerably larger than any others in the country, ranging from forty to sixty couples, plus Don and Heather and a 'guest couple' who they ask to help lead the weekend. From the list of topics covered in two separate years, it would appear the sort of thing that couples could attend year after year. Most other weekends do not offer this rotation of topics. Also, Don and Heather do not cram nearly as much into the weekend as most, making this by far the most relaxing weekend on offer. In fact, it may be more accurate to define this ministry as an in-residence seminar on marriage rather than a Christian marriage weekend in the sense that has been described in this chapter.

We have attempted to give an objective sketch of the

many types of weekend available, without being either condoning or condemning. As you can see, there is a vast range of types and styles, and even depth. Biblical content ranges from the type of material presented in this book all the way to the completely secular. There are some fairly charismatic weekends, and some where the non-charismatic would be more comfortable. Most weekends are packed full. The organizers have a lot of material to present and they try to structure a commensurate amount of time for couples to communicate on each issue presented. This all boils down to hard work, but we have never had anyone seriously accuse us of working them too hard. On the contrary, they feel that it is well worth the effort. We think that most who design and conduct marriage weekends feel a responsibility to give their clients their money's worth, which means presenting well-planned, cogent material and creating an atmosphere conducive to communication. There is also an overriding ambition to avoid superficiality after the promise has been made to take couples deeper into their relationship with each other and the Lord. For instance, Marriage Encounter's slogan, 'The 44 hours that will change your life', has less chance of being true the more the 'holiday' atmosphere is increased.

Marriage weekends are not foolproof. Even on the most structured weekends, no one can make you communicate with your partner (if there was a way, we would try it!). Some couples do manage to keep the whole marriage weekend at arm's length—and each other as well; but it does not make much sense to pay out the price of the weekend and give up 44 hours, and not try to get a return value.

There is a saying that 'you can lead a horse to water, but you can't make him drink'. You can't—but you can greatly encourage it by putting salt in his oats. That is one of the main purposes of the talks on Christian marriage weekends, to 'salt the oats' of couples, so that they will communicate in the allotted times and hopefully develop a life-long habit of communicating.

We have raised the idea of getting your money's-worth, and quite naturally the cost is a very obvious concern. Hopefully, this book will still be read long after inflation has out-dated any figures we can give, but there is a way to keep in touch with this cost. The main cost of the Weekend is obviously the cost of accommodation in a Christian conference centre or a hotel. At the time of writing, it costs approximately £50 to £75 per couple for a weekend in a Christian conference centre. There are probably as many various ways of meeting expenses for Christian marriage weekends as there are varieties of weekends. We ourselves charge simply what the conference centre charges us per couple (including VAT*), which obviously does not cover our expenses. There is the cost of accommodation for the team couples, approximately £2-worth of handouts per couple, plus a lot of organization and administrative expenses. Consequently, during our last session we point out that there is a basket at the back of the room where contributions could be made to defray some of these additional expenses. Even with this, we seldom 'break even'; but like other people who operate marriage weekends, we are a registered charity, and people make donations that eventually cover this. Some weekends make a flat charge which covers all operating expenses, and others work entirely on a donation basis. The bottom line is that these operating costs have got to be made in some way, or the charity cannot continue to function. In determining the cost of a Weekend, a good rule-of-thumb would probably be the cost of the centre (our most expensive to date is £60 including VAT), and added to this, about 10% or 15% to

*You may question the requirement of VAT, since there are provisions for educational courses to be exempt. The fact is that Marriage Weekends are educational, and this education will save the Government in the long run through saved marriages. However, seminars given from a Christian world view are all too easily considered 'religious' and not 'educational'. If you think this is absurd please write to your MP (and send the authors a copy as well). We would like to see the Government set up a separate category for anything designed to save marriages.

cover costs. It may seem like a lot to spend £60 or £70 for a Marriage Weekend, but it is very small compared with the cost of holidays and we think that most couples who have attended a Marriage Weekend would agree that it was the best money they had ever spent.

The price of a Marriage Weekend is also a wonderful gift to give to another couple who may not be able to afford such a Weekend. Also, it is an excellent policy for churches to subsidize their couples going on a marriage weekend. Our own church pays 50% of the cost for any couple that wants to go on a weekend. Many couples donate money so that there may be funds available for any couple who cannot afford to pay and have no church or friends to back them up. We certainly have such a 'scholarship fund', and we are pleased to be able to say that we have never turned anyone away because of lack of funds. We know for a fact that many other marriage weekends operate in exactly the same way regarding scholarship funds.

There are two categories of couples who definitely would not benefit from a marriage weekend. The first is the couple whose marriage is in dire straits. They would require at least two or three sessions of counselling before they would be able to benefit from such a weekend. The second category is the couple who are so insecure that admitting there is room for improvement is tantamount to admitting to failure.

I have in my hand a letter from Dr James Dobson discussing the Marriage Encounter that he attended with his wife Shirley. It would be very easy for a person like Dr Dobson, who writes many books on marriage and relationships, to feel that he would have little to gain from such a weekend. Indeed in his letter he wrote that he was 'quite frankly, expecting little that would benefit Shirley and me. We have a beautiful, open relationship and did not feel we needed communicative help. *I was wrong!*'

No couple is immune from communication breakdown; often it is on a very low level and can go unrecognized for years. We always shudder when we hear someone who says, 'We certainly don't need that.' Somehow we get the 'gut-level' feeling that they are exactly the couple who need it most.

Appendix

Association for Marriage Enrichment:

    c/o Westminster Pastoral Foundation
    23 Kensington Square
    London W8 5HN

    Tel: 071 937 6956

Care and Counsel:

    St Mary Magdalene Church
    Holloway Road
    London N7 8LT

    Tel: 071 609 4545

The Staffords:

    Roy and Jan Stafford
    4 Elder Road
    Ware
    Herts SG12 7JF

    Tel: 0920 462410

Good News Crusade:

> 17 High Cross Street
> St Austell
> Cornwall PL25 4AN
>
> Tel: 0726 72282

Marriage Encounter
Anglican Expression:

> Keith and Cheryl Elkins
> 7 Lyons Close
> Ruddington
> Nottingham NG11 6BQ
>
> Tel: 0602 215172

Marriage Encounter
Baptist Expression:

> The Revd Norman Barr
> 12 South Street
> Leighton Buzzard
> Bedfordshire LU7 8NT
>
> Tel: 0525 371312

Marriage Encounter
Catholic Expression:

> Bob and Flora Bell
> 6 Cotton Field Road
> Withington
> Manchester M20 9QW
>
> Tel: 061 434 7303

Marriage Fulfilment:

> David and Joyce Huggett
> 18 Lenton Road
> The Park
> Nottingham NG7 1DU
>
> Tel: 0602 411383

Marriage Refreshment:

> Michael and Gillian Warren
> Banks Farm
> Barcombe
> Lewes
> East Sussex BN8 5DY
>
> Tel: 0273 400205

Note: The fact that the work of Michael and Gillian Warren is not discussed in the epilogue is an oversight. We have only become acquainted with them since the first printing of this book, they have, however, been ministering to marriages since 1984. The cosy marriage weekends which they run in their own home never exceed 10 couples but have won them high regard in evangelical circles.

Marriage Review:

> Ron and Violet Holmes
> 38 Park Drive
> Ingatestone
> Essex CM4 9DT
>
> Tel: 0277 353117

Mission to Marriage: (Dave and Joyce Ames)

> Mission to Marriage
> 20 Mill Street
> Mildenhall
> Suffolk IP28 7DP
>
> Tel: 0638 713047

* The Association of Biblical Counsellors:

> Townsend Chambers
> Amherst Hill
> Sevenoaks
> Kent TN13 2EL
>
> Tel: 0732 460625

* Note: The Association of Biblical Counsellors does not conduct Marriage Weekends, but can most likely provide the name and address, etc of counsellors who are prepared to counsel from a totally biblical framework. This is a very young organization of which we are members. The ABC is working very hard to train, recognize and provide a directory for biblical counselling referral throughout Great Britain.

Looking Up The Aisle?

by Dave & Joyce Ames

It has been said that more preparation goes into a driving licence than a marriage licence. This is a workbook—designed to be used by couples to work through together. As they do so they will discover more about each other's priorities and goals in life, so that they have an adequate basis on which to make a decision about the commitment of marriage.

'The realistic approach of *Looking Up The Aisle?* will, I am sure, give a very strong foundation to many marriages.'

David Alton MP

'A concise, clear and well-structured workbook. It covers a lot of ground in a short time without making any omissions or assumptions that would be unhelpful.'

Andy Butcher
former Editor, *Christian Family* magazine

DAVE AND JOYCE AMES have been married for thirty-six years. They run *Mission to Marriage* seminars and are the authors of *Second Honeymoon*.

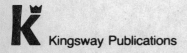

Kingsway Publications

Marriage—The Early Years

by Ian & Ruth Coffey

Marriage means adjustment.

Emotionally—learning how to build a friendship together and adjust to another person's way of doing things.

Physically—discovering sexuality as a gift from God and learning how the best lovers give rather than take!

Socially—building a home together where others can find hospitality and friendship.

Spiritually—growing together in God and discovering your place in the local church.

It's all an exciting new challenge, and this book aims to equip you for your new life together.

IAN & RUTH COFFEY have been married for fifteen years, and have four sons. Ian is a Baptist minister and Field Director of the Evangelical Alliance; Ruth is a nurse and home-maker.

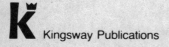

Kingsway Publications

Marriage As God Intended

by Selwyn Hughes

'We have never had an argument in the whole of our marriage,' said the husband.
'How did you accomplish that?' asked the counsellor.
'We just don't talk.'

Communication is only one of the problem areas faced by married couples—there can be many other difficulties that cause us to fall short of God's perfect plan.

This book offers help—not only with specific problems, but for improving what is already good and healthy.

There are chapters on:
> relationships with parents and in-laws
> who's the head of the family?
> sexual difficulties
> the temptation to adultery
> divorce and remarriage

Selwyn Hughes is highly respected as a leading marriage guidance counsellor. Here he draws on his many years' experience as both husband and counsellor, blending biblical principles with practical suggestions on how to let God keep your marriage at its best.

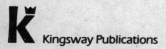

Kingsway Publications

Man to Man about Women

by James Dobson

It's time to be honest about ourselves. Today's society is involved in a pathetic search for personal pleasure.

Women's Lib is not so much a movement as a cry from the heart to be understood—as a God-given human being. Dr James Dobson attempts to set the matter right. He's a psychologist, husband and father. His writings are not theoretical but born of practical involvement in the problems confronted by women.

This book is for men and women—written by a man for men, but its aim is to understand one of God's greatest gifts to man—a woman!

Some of this book's topics—
  What causes depression in women
  The effect of fatigue and time pressure
  Sex machine or sex partner
  Menstrual and physiological problems
and a host of other down-to-earth factors.

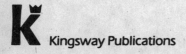

Kingsway Publications